FORBIDDEN REVOLUTIONS

Gospel & Culture is a movement of Christians from many different Churches and traditions. We are united by our commitment to Jesus Christ and by a determination to engage with today's culture and to communicate the gospel to it.

We work together to create resources which help Christians relate their faith to the real world. They include. . .

- Touring lectures, workshops and weekend conferences. Led by some of the Church's leading thinkers and communicators, these are designed to sharpen and inform the faith of Christians and local churches.

- Books such as this one, tapes, occasional papers, and our regular newsletter.

- Our twice-yearly journal, *Leading Light*, which tackles the major cultural issues facing Christians today. Written with wit and style, and in clear, accessible language, *Leading Light* is a valuable resource for anyone who wants to communicate the gospel in our culture.

For more information about Gospel & Culture and *Leading Light*, please write to Lavinia Harvey, Gospel & Culture, Dept of Theology & Religious Studies, King's College London, The Strand, London WC2R 2LS.

FORBIDDEN REVOLUTIONS

*

*Pentecostalism in Latin America and
Catholicism in Eastern Europe*

*

DAVID MARTIN

First published 1996
SPCK
Holy Trinity Church
Marylebone Road
London NW1 4DU

British Library Cataloguing in Publication Data
A catalogue record for this book is available from
the British Library.

ISBN 0–281–04999–8

Typeset by The Midlands Book Typesetting
Company, Loughborough, Leicestershire.
Printed in Great Britain by The Longdunn Press, Bristol

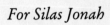

For Silas Jonah

CONTENTS

*

Preface

*

This short book is substantially the F.D. Maurice lectures given at King's College, London University, in May-June 1991, and repeated in 1992 at St Paul's College, Sydney University. I revised the lectures slightly in November 1993 and again substantially in September 1995, so this is a layered production.

I want to express very warm thanks to King's College for allowing me to be part of a distinguished lineage, and to Professor Colin Gunton and his colleagues for the added hospitality of a visiting professorship. To that I add equal thanks to St Paul's College for their great kindness. Thanks are also due to Dr Lew Wheeler and the Australian Prayer Book Society for underpinning much of the financial needs of the trip, and also for welcoming me to speak at several enjoyable meetings.

As ever, I owe a great deal to Peter Berger and the Institute for the Study of Economic Culture for financial and other support in the gathering of material lying behind the discussion of Latin America.

The material used here is not footnoted in the standard academic manner, and I've relied on memory for much of the information. Since these were lectures, I have allowed myself to use a discursive, illustrative, and even a literary approach in handling sociological issues. There is also some repetition between chapters to re-establish themes, given that there was a somewhat different audience for each lecture. Those not specially interested in sociological issues may prefer to travel lightly over the first part of Chapter 1.

This little book has something of an interim character. With regard to the Latin American material, it comes between my *Tongues of Fire* (Basil Blackwell 1990) and a second book that should appear under the imprint of Princeton University Press. With regard to the European material, it comes between my *A General Theory of Secularization* (Basil Blackwell 1978) and a projected volume for Oxford University Press on religion in Europe. It also overlaps my Sarum Lectures on Religion and War given at Oxford University in January-March 1995 and to be published by OUP.

In a way these lectures are a reflection on why Catholicism has sustained losses in Latin America and has outlasted communism in Eastern Europe. It suggests that both phenomena occur for a similar reason: the margins of society (Pentecostalism in Latin America and Catholicism in Eastern Europe) can be powerful solvents of established monopoly power. 'The Kingdom' can hit back – peaceably, which is not an inappropriate theme for F.D. Maurice lectures.

DAVID MARTIN

1

Why and how the two revolutions were forbidden

✻

One needs to begin with two assertions that complement one another. The first is that the sociology of
religion is not primarily about marginal phenomena. If
we set aside Western Europe as the exceptional case in
our contemporary world, you cannot make much sense
of what is seriously going forward without some
understanding of religion. Everywhere religion impinges
on politics, though not necessarily through so-called
religious parties. The natural partner of the sociology of
religion is political sociology, each dealing with specific
kinds of power and with the way these impinge and
overlap, and even combine. That means you need a capa-
cious understanding of power, including, for example,
the condensed sign language of religion and the personal
transformations that religion brings about and the
implicit models of behaviour and organization it generates.

The second assertion is that religion remains central

to our understanding, even though, through the process of secularization – and, in particular, differentiation – it is no longer united to the state and is becoming decreasingly associated with political parties. Its primary social location is culture, and if one believes culture to be literally an inconsequential marginal and private matter, then one may say religion has been marginalized. However, as will be asserted more than once in this chapter, culture is not merely a derivative sphere that picks up impulses from the supposed 'motors' of change, but one that autonomously generates its own transformations. It sends back messages to the centre. The two revolutions that form the subject of this book have affected (or are affecting) the centre. In the case of the changes of 1989–90, they touched closely on the public realm, and in the case of evangelical expansions in Latin America they bear on the possibility and likely texture of any future civil society.

Why is it so difficult to make out this case given that it is (in my view) highly plausible? What militates against its acceptance? One reason is to be found in the all-embracing paradigms of progress and of secularization discussed in the latter part of this chapter. The other – not unconnected – has to do with our categories and vocabulary. Our categories and vocabulary are part and parcel of the standard rhetoric of sociology, which is closely intertwined with the standard rhetoric of the contemporary Western intelligentsia. For that matter, it is all too closely linked to the jargon of business organization and political discourse.

By suggesting that sociology uses a misleading rhetoric I am not suggesting that it is not a form of knowledge. It defers to the evidence and is controlled by data – that is, by things that are given and not selectively plucked from the air. It also works by standard rules of inference and seeks out such generalities as may exist in the social world. At the same time, it is also concerned with a narrative within which individuals act and project. Moreover, there is a plethora of possible kinds of evidence and frames of reference from which it may select. As for its categories, they do not comprise demarcated units or blocks of material, but fluid foci with imprecise names and persistently overlapping boundaries. Sociological theories are more or less plausible interpretations, and their impact depends in considerable measure on how categories and vocabularies are expanded or contracted. Because these categories and vocabularies are embedded in our ordinary descriptive and normative language, they are coloured by association and emit auras of approval and disapproval.

Thus a sociological case when made out is not only comprised of evidence, rigorous inference and hypotheses, but also affected by the range of the categories selected and the associations trailed by the vocabulary. This is true even in those cases where authors seek to eliminate all colour and deploy vocabularies with an aura of impersonality and objectivity as, for example, when they talk about 'behaviours'. It follows that sociology is analysis framed in a rhetoric that has interesting resemblances to advocacy in a court of law. If you read sociological articles and books you see how extraordinarily careful authors have to be in the use of rhetoric lest they strike the wrong note, and how closely their style resembles the handling of a brief. (To this one may add a generous use of inverted commas to suggest arcane or special meanings, or to scare off criticism, and the use of passive tenses and roundabout locutions to imply impersonal process rather than human agency. The style of sociology principally derives from its theoretical basis and *not* from sociologists' lack of education.)

Rhetoric and its attendant vocabulary identifies and focuses. However, it also distorts, and nowhere more subtly and pervasively than with respect to the matters about to be discussed. The vocabularies that do most damage in the case of the revolutions in Latin America and Eastern Europe are the false polarities of left and right, liberal and fundamentalist, political and apolitical, cultural and structural, to which I might add central and marginal, and active and derivative. It is these, along with their background apparatus, that forbade the occurrence of these revolutions.

Take first the vocabulary of left and right. The world is not for ever divided into rival poles according to the shape of the French Chamber of Deputies. Movements cannot be docketed along such one-dimensional continua. The problem with our use of 'left' and 'right' immediately emerges once you consider the contemporary use of the term 'radical'. It has travelled a long way from its nineteenth-century uses, because 'radical' in the strict sense of 'going to the root of the problem' depends on what you are being radical about and who or what is your historical opponent. The same problem is illustrated by the way communists used to be located on the left, but now in the Soviet Union they are located on the right. Many contemporary liberals are exercised over how to locate communism because they are trapped between an older identification that linked it to protest against exploitation, and the perceived realities of communist regimes that identify it as one of the most exploitative and dehumanizing systems of our time.

Just as the world no longer reflects the French Chamber of Deputies, so it is not for ever divided up in terms that reflect the struggles of American religious conservatives with liberals. Here the main casualty is the term 'fundamentalist'. It seems we are in danger of using the word 'fundamentalist' to cover every form of communal fanaticism as well as several very different versions of conservative religion, and then of fusing both together under the influence of a liberal panic.

How, then, do these political vocabularies of left and right, radical and conservative, cripple our understanding of the movements now under consideration? Partly they do so because they are embedded in the social metaphysic of progress that works by bi-polar contrasts (with religion consigned to the static and evanescent) and that also constricts ideological space by making it unilinear. Movements can do other things beside contribute or fail to contribute to the secular utopias and political epiphanies that once dominated Western expectation. Even if these are now discredited, they still inform our desire to map where people are, to give the right names to movements, and to deploy rhetorics defining what is 'positive' and what is 'sinister'. Worse than that, a new movement need only display one characteristic conventionally designated as 'sinister', such as a vigorous deployment of authority, and it is discredited by the associations automatically called up. You have only to take a stadium for a large-scale meeting and you are setting yourself up for Fascist comparisons.

With this echo box of resonances in operation with respect to these two revolutions it becomes easy to miss the one thing necessary, which is the break-up of the hegemony of ideological power and the creation of autonomous space for the egalitarian exercise of personal and spiritual gifts. Yet this is precisely what the small cells of Pentecostal believers represent and it is replete with implications. It is also what is represented by the small cells within the major Churches of what was the 'Eastern bloc'. These are radical because they lie among the grass-roots potentials for cultural change. One does not have to search for some *other* feature that fits better with our own local and historic models of how change really ought to come about.

Nor need radical be always opposed to conservative. For example, in contemporary Britain there is a creeping managerialism in every sphere, including Church and university, and there are those who seek to conserve certain values of autonomy as well as to find vehicles for their continuous creation. That is radical conservation. In a similar way, the movements in Latin America can simultaneously seek to revise old values, such as the macho personality, and seek to conserve ideals of familial solidarity and mutuality. Thus the ethos of Pentecos-talism and the ethos of Catholic moralism may each in their different ways seek to conserve what they regard as worthwhile, and promote radical initiatives to renew respect for the intrinsic worth of life. The conservation of the personal in societies such as now exist in Latin America and in Eastern Europe is not a side-issue to be consigned to an impotent private sphere. In that respect, thinkers and politicians like Vaclav Havel have their social priorities right.

There are many countries where the whole of society has been so dehumanized and its language about itself so debased that to conserve a personal world against relentless encroachment is a radical achievement. If one looks at the iconography of evangelical churches in Latin America with their clear streams, bright flowers and protective shepherds, the desire for images of cleansing and of the human and familial scale is evident. It is the same radical conservation that has been achieved in the dark iconic interiors of thousands of Central and Eastern European churches. Tending the lights and burnishing their containers is not the 'irrelevant' activity of the female, the old and the female old. *Being* is a form of *doing*, and it is a macho social 'science' which, inter alia, prevents us from seeing how and when that can be so.

As for the terms 'left' and 'right', they too depend on time and context. So what is that context? In Latin America, the Roman Catholic Church remains for the most part aligned with social conservation of various kinds through being tied in to the social hierarchies of almost every Latin American nation. The base communities challenge that alignment even though they have been reined in by the hierarchy of recent years, or else partly bypassed by partial shifts to democracy. The older usages of 'left' and 'right' still make some kind of sense here, especially given the historic replication of French and Spanish patterns of clericals versus anti-clericals. Yet when it comes to evangelical groups they do not really fit these polarized patterns, though being anti-Catholic and anti-Marxist restricts their choices and has led some pastorates to shelter under – and even to shore up – military regimes. But their apolitical withdrawals in some contexts and their groping for a political channel of expression in others could just as easily presage a fragmentation in which the old polarities cease to act as rival magnets of adhesion or analytic understanding. They could be part of a crumbling of older alignments and represent a shift towards interest groups and towards voluntary associations. These might well perform beneficial roles in the creation of social capital, and in time they could find a voice among a wider medley of voices. They would be radical, but not on the left. Such distinctions are possible, and increasingly they acquire social purchase. 'The old order changeth giving place to new' and it is our own 'natural' orderings of the world that belong to history.

Perhaps that is clearer in the context of Eastern Europe. During the revolutionary period of 1988–90, the communist power elites (and their vast military establishments) were cast by commentators as being on the right. The religiously infiltrated movements for greater liberty and opportunity for varied political expression were, therefore, located on 'the left'. To some extent, those terminologies are still in place. For example, the resurgent 'National' (indeed Imperial) Communism of Russia still counts as right wing. But are economically neo-liberal movements also to be located on the right, or do they belong on the left or somewhere in a more multi-dimensional ordering of political space? One notices that the pragmatic ex-communists of Eastern Europe are gradually reacquiring a left-wing label simply because they challenge recent post-revolutionary governing coalitions. However, they turn out in the main to be movements for slowing up change. Like everyone else, they are under the inhibiting aegis of the IMF. Does 'left wing' nowadays mean no more than a pragmatic curb on radical change?

And what of the religious elements now that they have

largely separated out from the radical political movements to which they once lent such potent symbolism? Some have shifted back to a role in the creation of social capital. Others are now associated with attempts to protect the culture of threatened minorities – for example, the Hungarians in Romania. Those engaged in such attempts deploy the language of human rights, but this kind of cultural conservation used to be labelled as on 'the right'. Is it necessarily so? In the West, movements for cultural conservation (as least as pursued in the Third World) are often a preoccupation of intellectuals on the left. Could it be that what is a 'left-wing cause' among the Aymara of Bolivia is a right-wing cause among the Greeks of Albania, and is virtually unlocatable among the Turks of Bulgaria? In short, context is crucial. The old alignments increasingly mislead and misidentify.

As for 'fundamentalist', it is rapidly becoming an all-purpose pejorative in the vocabulary of liberal moral panic. Curiously enough, those who now emerge as violent religious fanatics in North Africa and elsewhere were only yesterday applauded as the damned of the earth, and their violence regarded as exemplary. At that time they were Marxists and hence on the left. Yet once the old terminology is converted into a Koranic vocabulary, these same movements – and, in many cases, these same people – wander in a political dimension we do not easily understand and are recategorized for convenience under the umbrella term of 'fundamentalist'. It seems that a fundamentalist is now someone who wants to force the rest of society to obey a hegemonic system of religious law and who leaves bombs on trains. One can only speculate how the IRA might be categorized if it showed more overt signs of a genuinely Catholic piety or of the

Catholic intégrisme that is still influential in the Irish Republic. Somehow they have held on to a semi-respectable location in the political field through being vaguely left, in spite of simultaneously representing a 'Catholic nationalist' cause and being fanatical and violent. Why is their fanaticism not fundamentalist according to current usage?

The trouble with the term 'fundamentalist' is that it includes (Southern) Baptists who pioneered the separation of Church and state (and often repudiate the term) along with Pentecostals in Latin America, Nigeria and Zimbabwe, and militant Islamic groups in Algeria, Pakistan, Egypt, Iran or wherever. But, as already indicated, the Pentecostals in Latin America represent the creation of autonomous spiritual space *over against* comprehensive systems. They are the power of fission and are, moreover, resolutely non-violent. Indeed, they are constantly sneered at for their 'passive' peaceability by comparison with guerrillas. Islamic fundamentalists work in an entirely opposed direction since they create autonomous space explicitly in order to eliminate that space. Why are such antithetical forms of religion grouped together?

Once the term 'fundamentalist' is applied to Latin American Pentecostals, it identifies them by a characteristic that is marginal to understanding what they are about. It is true that they take a conservative view of Scripture and of morality; but that by no means informs their social and theological being as it does the 'fundamentalist' wing of the Southern (or Northern) Baptists. Of course, they have a conservative understanding of the Bible, but that is not remotely sufficient to characterize their essential thrust, which is the free and democratic availability of the gifts of the Spirit. *That* is what animates a Pentecostalist. It is also what helps to ensure that they divide and subdivide and so increase the range of options and prevent any serious hegemonic ambition. What they define themselves *against* is not 'east coast liberals', but the priestly and the formulaic. It is, incidentally, quite curious that the Catholics and Orthodox of Eastern Europe never attract the term 'fundamentalist' even when they are theologically very conservative. Opus Dei might attract the term, but that is about the limit of its deployment with respect to conservative ecclesiastical Christianity. Does this mean, then, that 'fundamentalism' is only such when its origins are fairly recent? Once again, we have illustration of how bi-polar antitheses travel away from their original historical and local context and become increasingly unhelpful.

Parallel problems arise for the analysis of these two movements from the supposed polarity between 'political' and 'apolitical'. In this respect, we commit the sin of 'ethnocentricity', but pardon ourselves because our sin is committed in the name of progress. The fact is that we – and I include myself – are (nearly) all of us comfortable members of the political and politicized classes in the West. Our conception of what counts as truly political turns around sophisticated and extended discourse about social structural change as this takes place in the sphere of political process and public events.

The truth is that most people in the world are too poor for our kind of politics, and in any case they live in a context where our categorizations do not necessarily apply. The nearly half a billion people of Latin America offer a prime instance. Most of them belong to underclasses that struggle for survival while corrupt and remote political classes wrangle over their heads for the spoils of state and nation. In such a situation, evangelicals and Pentecostals are political because they try to alter what is in their capacity to alter, beginning with themselves, their families and congregations. They bind themselves together on rafts of discipline and hope and, so far as is possible, cut themselves off from the corruption and violence all around them, most evidently in the political sphere. They engage, as Rowan Ireland has pointed out, in a politics of culture, and they show what Roger Lancaster has called the courage of 'creative despair'.[1] These two anthropologists – one a liberal and a Catholic, and the other a Marxist – have done much to break the mould of our preconceptions.

A secondary by-product of the polarity we set up between political and apolitical is that we now set the Roman Catholic Church, and especially its base communities, firmly in the sphere of the political. The point has been made above, and it is correct in the sense that the Roman Catholic Church has always been political and a massive presence in the polis. However, we are certainly misled if we suppose that the bulk of the Roman Catholic Church has been radicalized. As is indicated later, the base communities are for the most part devotional, and, in so far as they are political, they mainly concern themselves with local issues. The Marxism of the early phase, some of which was bizarre, has abated; and all this is true quite apart from the influence of John Paul II. Of course, where lay catechists and priests stand up against the tyrants of their little fields that is heroic, and Madeleine Adriance has recently documented instances of that in the Amazon basin. I am simply saying that this high-profile political action is not everyday reality.

If this seems to anticipate the substance of the argument to follow, it does nevertheless illustrate very well the distorting effects of our categories. We of the Western intelligentsia live in a world where moral judgements have been tied up within political attitudes, and our public arena consists of a struggle for rectitude between rival rhetorics. In that struggle we sort out good guys and bad guys with the aid of these categories, and then project our judgements on to other cultures.

A further problem in sorting out people politically is that, for the most part, we only listen to those who are like ourselves. That is precisely how we have come to accept the self-assessment of liberation theologians rather than explore the everyday realities of the base communities. These theologians write in our media and speak in our lecture rooms because they share our language; thus we hear their voice. And the principle of hope *demands* somebody in Latin America perform according to their eloquent script; sometimes they do, as in rural Brazil. But as for the rest of the people, they are merely spoken *about*. They are described and categorized as good or bad, political or apolitical, left or right, but we never hear their own voices and would not dream of taking them seriously if we did. After all, it is we who are the agents of history, we who know where we are and what is going on, whereas they are ignorant armies of flailing somnambulists.

All this means that in many areas, and particularly with respect to religion, our boasted relativism is a sham. Part of what I attempt to do, particularly in the Latin American material presented here, is to evoke a world other than our own and show how it works. Of course, part of the problem is that the world evoked is not quite foreign enough. Were it comprised of ancestor worshippers in Vietnam or shamans in Siberia, we would suspend judgement and not impose our categories. In this case, though, it looks like an affiliate of a religion we already know and understand how to place intellectually and socially. We have, so to speak, already done our thinking about that, and may now proceed on automatic pilot and guided by articles in the Sunday supplements.

In this discussion of the uses and abuses of terms like 'political' and 'apolitical' the focus has been on Latin America, but it is also important not to use too restrictive an understanding of what is really political in Eastern (and Central) Europe. In dealing with the revolutionary changes of 1989–90 I have stressed that they in large measure advanced behind the banners of religion. In a major political trial in Lithuania prior to the changes, the defence was conducted in the classic language of Christian martyrdom. In the early phase of the events in western Ukraine, one was apprised of something afoot by the appearance of religious banners in the streets.

This is not in the main because religion is an implicit channel for political impulses where these are banned in their explicit form, though there is some truth in that. It is because the specifically religious mode of action, which is simultaneously intimate and immediate and on the horizon of eternity, has its moment in the public square. At a particular phase in the movement for change, religious signs can convey certain very broad sentiments of human and civic dignity and integrity. There comes a time when a condensed religious symbol that may have no verbal content whatever, and certainly articulates no precise programme, serves to announce a presence and a desire for a new order. Once the concrete possibility of a new order opens up, it then becomes a question of precise dispositions of power, and at that point the religious signs revert to the background and are once more held in reserve.

That is why the changes were mostly brought about by peaceable processions rather than by mob violence. It was as if the liturgical spirit that normally winds through the covered aisles of churches had walked out into the open air. Moreover, the leaders of these processions were often completely apolitical animals who (like the signs they carried) emerged for a phase and then returned to the background. Walesa and Tokes are exceptions to this, but it was true of many others at that time. One Orthodox priest told me of being present in the crowd that formed in the main square of Sibiu, Romania, at the time when some seventy people, mainly students, were shot down by the Securitate. Within a year he retired from the political arena in disgust, and now barely reads newspapers. Nevertheless, what occurred in that square was a defining moment, and in its meaning and consequences it was political. When it comes to religious action, our ordinary divisions of political and apolitical have to be stretched and revised.

The final misleading polarity is that between culture and structure, where the former is seen as derivative and passive and the latter as the arena of effective power and political action. Religion is supposedly confined to the former. It is treated as a reflection and never brings anything about from its own innate resources. On this account, religion merely lives in people's private consciousness or, at most, stays in the ambit of congregations and churches. The subjective condition of people with religious faith is irrelevant to the dynamic of real action. The only exception to this appears to be their capacity to do harm, in which respect they are held to be remarkably potent.

The argument of what follows is quite to the contrary. The cultural margin (or rather the margin we call culture) can affect the so-called centre. The potentials built up and stored in culture and the slow uneventful changes that occur there are, in the long run, rich in consequence. They really make a difference in respect of things that really matter. Culture is the stuff of the longue durée, persisting over centuries, and it is that long durance that counts. The implicit models created in the cultural sphere, whether we are thinking of the decentralized autonomy of independency in the seventeenth century or the participatory style of Pentecostalism or of the cells within the Church in (former) Czechoslovakia, Hungary, the GDR and Romania, are rich in implication, and in their capacity to induct into new forms of behaviour.

It is, of course, true that the Christian religion has been relieved of (or taken leave of) its association with the state and even with political parties. That is a kind of marginalization, but it means religion gains certain freedoms and loses certain constraints. Margins can transmit messages to the centre, sometimes by their mere existence, and in the long run, as in Eastern Europe, the centres may partially implode.

Inevitably, the theme of marginalization introduces the theory of secularization. It is one of the components in the theory of secularization that marginalization is also privatization and hence inconsequentiality. I have advanced many criticisms of the theory of secularization, with regards to its conceptual incoherence, its ideological roots, its shuffling of criteria to cope with recalcitrant evidence and its unilinear view of history, but concern here is focused almost entirely on that sub-section of the theory concerned with marginalization. I accept that there has been marginalization, but I do not believe that that consigns religion to the domain of mere marginalia. In that respect, I concur entirely with a recent book by José Casanova entitled *Public Religions in the Modern World*.[2] The two cases here presented of power active at the margin impinge on the problematic of secularization and serve to complement the various instances cited by Casanova of the role of religion (which, as it happens, include Poland).

Before dealing more directly with the real relevance of secularization, I want to make two points concerning the effects of the theory itself in the West and in the East. In the West it acts as an implicit guide and censor on what we permit ourselves to see and in the East it was the guiding spirit of an explicit programme to enforce secularization as a political programme.

With regard to secularization as providing an implicit guide as to what we are enabled to see, that does not mean we are, or were, oblivious to the events of 1989–90. We knew about them just as we know about Islam in Algeria, because they were politically eventful. At the same time, the cultural elements present within and behind those events were virtually invisible. I give an example, which is indicative even though it occurred after rather than before the events of 1989–90. The Pope's visit to Lithuania did not figure at all on Western television news, though it was shown (after protest?) on a feature programme. His visit was an extraordinary occasion summoning up the history of a people and its resistance over decades, but so far as the media were concerned it did not happen. Or again, it was reported that the initial disturbances in Timisoara had something to do with a priest, but the person concerned, Lazlo Tokes, was in fact a Hungarian Reformed pastor.

Naturally there are many reasons why cameras cannot be present apart from blindness, ignorance and selectivity, but it remains the case that the absence of the camera turns genuinely crucial occasions into non-events. It is evident that Western reporters when they visit the sites of important changes do not know how to recognize the religious aspect, let alone interpret it. The instances I refer to in the chapter on Eastern Europe are in part from memory simply because references to them were tucked away in obscure corners or I found them out through personal conversation and contacts. (How this works in Latin America I know only too well. Time and again I have been asked by television personnel to provide documentation of specifically right-wing activities of evangelicals, and on one occasion was told that contrary instances were of no interest.) In a way, of course, this skewed perception could count as genuine evidence of secularization in the West. The existence of such ideological blinkers itself counts in favour of the proposition.

However, secularization in the East has worked rather differently since the implicit skew in perception in the West is there an explicit programme to implement secularization as a component of state policy. To redeploy Hegel, those who refused to co-operate with 'history' were to be dragged. According to Marxist theory, religion was placed in a past historical phase and was not to leak into the present. If the present age did not come to birth by a natural pregnancy, then there would have to be a Caesarian operation. The theory declared that the time when religion could act was over, and in the present era it could only re-act and be reactionary. God had become otiose. When I visited what was in essence the Department of Ideology in Sofia University in 1967, I was told (by the late Professor Ochavkov) that Bulgaria was the exemplary instance of the advance of history and social development. By contrast, Poland was a case of chronic retardation, and in due course 'Anglia' would catch up with Bulgaria. These remarks were in themselves highly significant because they illustrated the practical union of communism with nationalism.

Even more pervasive than Marxist theorizing about religion are the broad notions deriving from the Enlightenment. I certainly do not count myself among those who today repudiate the Enlightenment, since we clearly stand on its shoulders even to review its defects. Yet there is an important sense in which the Enlightenment project, like every other, simultaneously focuses our vision and restricts it. The presuppositions of the Enlightenment, more particularly of the atypical and irreligious French Enlightenment, have entered into our way of thinking, and have contributed to a serious disability in understanding religion and its continuing ability to be consequential. The debate now is whether the Enlightenment project, complete with all its ancillary baggage about religion, goes on to conquer the world from its European base or whether its secular messianism is tempered and the lights of religion and reason become complementary rather than antagonistic. It is at least evident that the ideology of reason is as capable of persecution and oppression as the religion of love. The 'infamy' once predicated of religion alone is shared by all the other great systems of thought. It inheres in human sociation as such. The year 1989 may have been a sign that the trajectory of 1789 had completed its course and come to rest.

The encounter of religion with the Enlightenment has another history germane to the two revolutions here discussed, and that is the particular outcome of their clash country by country. These outcomes run through a wide gamut of possibilities. In Latin America they extend from the virtual triumph of the Church in Colombia to its virtual defeat in Uruguay, and in Europe they extend from its triumph in Poland to its defeat in France. It is these outcomes that switch the broad tendencies of secularization one way or another, or even cancel them. They also to some extent set the terms within which evangelical religion in Latin America was able to expand more in some countries than others, and the terms within which religion in different Eastern European countries was able to exercise a role in the events of 1989–90. It now remains to review these outcomes, both in Latin America and Eastern Europe. We need to enquire as to their impact on the fragmentation of Catholicism in the former by Protestantism, and on the fragmentation of Marxism in the latter by Catholicism and other variants of the Christian religion.

In those instances in Latin America where the Church survived the conflicts in good heart and in addition had a native-born priesthood, as in Colombia, it was well placed to resist evangelical incursions. Where, as in Mexico, there was a stand-off, much might depend on local conditions that were unfavourable in south-east Mexico and favourable in south-west Mexico. Where, as in Uruguay, the Church was defeated and secularism established, the parlous state of religion *as such* might equally restrict Catholic revival and evangelical incursion. Where, as in Brazil and Guatemala, the Church was internally gutted without any secure and popular establishment of militant secularism, religion might develop outside its institutional frames and beyond any serious clerical control. This last outcome offered an open field to evangelical Christianity: the spiritual premiss remained intact, but the institutional cradle of established religion was cracked and weakened.

That is not to say that we can read off the opportunities for evangelical Christianity by making a tally of Catholic dispositions and conditions following the prolonged struggles with enlightened anti-clericalism. That is only one kind of relevant circumstance to be placed alongside, for example, levels of development, or the size and religious and cultural situation of non-Hispanic peoples, and so on. Indeed, *nothing* can be read off from any *particular* variable. South-east Brazil and Uruguay are both highly developed, but one is the world capital of Pentecostalism and the other the heartland of secularity.

What, then, of the parallel outcomes in Eastern and Central Europe – and, for that matter, Western Europe – because, after all, Europe remains to some extent a single universe of comparison. In France, which is the paradigm case of militant enlightenment in conflict with the Church Militant, the secular elites gained control of most of the commanding heights of the social order, though the conflict is now reduced to benevolent neutrality. The influence of the Church has also been weakening in neighbouring Belgium and Spain, and to a lesser extent in Italy. In short, the secularization story holds for Catholic Western Europe. In Eastern Europe, however, there have been two stages in the conflict: first, the radical and revolutionary anti-clericalism from the mid-nineteenth to the mid-twentieth century and, second, the overprinting of Soviet and/or communist domination. In the first stage, much turned on the relationship of religion to ethnic loyalty, which was strong in Poland, Lithuania, Croatia, Slovakia, etc., and weak in Moravia and Bohemia. It was the varied outcomes from this phase that partly set the terms for the struggle from 1948 to 1988. In that struggle, religion lost many sources of its own social reproduction, but gained from being the one remaining autonomous area against a combination of oppression and externally imposed government. The expulsion of the Church from the seats of power was much more sudden and complete than in Western Europe. The advantages of such an expulsion where government was oppressive far outweighed those gained by the slow extrusions and disentanglements of Western Europe. Even where Catholicism had been weak before communist rule, and seemed at first likely to go under, it gradually began to recover some ground. Where it was strong, it became the implicit mainstay of all resistance, democratic, nationalist or whatever. As for dissidence within the Church or fragmentation as a result of evangelical Protestantism, which would be a further manifestation of social differentiation, that did not really take off until the 1970s. It might marginally weaken the institutional Church, but it strengthened religion as such.

The result was that the pressure exercised by social differentiation against *all* inclusive and monopolistic systems of belief, which is one aspect of secularization, fell mainly on communism. Whereas in the West it slowly unhinged the overarching canopy of Catholicism and left it ambiguously implicated in decaying structures of power and socialization, in the East it rapidly unhinged political dogma. At the same time, it left religion unambiguously implicated in the bed-rock of historical continuity and ethnic memory. Even where, as in Romania, the Church was assimilated to the structure of power, and had been infiltrated and indoctrinated, the language of religion remained as a resource of the people at large. A strong internal dissidence rose through the huge organization known as the Lord's Army and a strong external dissidence through evangelical Protestantism, in this way providing a major echo of Latin America.

And so, by way of recapitulation, the long-term outcomes of the war between religion and enlightenment in Eastern Europe and in Latin America are important, though not *all*-important, for understanding the opportunities for evangelical Christianity in Latin America and the tide of conflict between the Church and communism in Eastern Europe. The contemporary situation in Eastern Europe, dramatized in the events of 1989–90, turned on the way communism took over the ideological establishment and so rendered itself vulnerable to the disintegrations of *all* such inclusive and dominating systems. Instead of the Church defensively retreating before social differentiation and ideological fragmentation, communism handed over to Christianity the advantages of the margin (to which it is by origin well adapted) as well as the opportunity to carry forward continuity and ethnicity. The net consequence is that as we step back and review the progress of social differentiation globally, we can observe at least four distinct trajectories in Christian cultures: Eastern Europe, Latin America, Western Europe and North America. If social differentiation is the working core of the theory of secularization, it takes at least four forms, which do not necessarily converge. That other variations occur in Islamic and other world cultures goes without saying. Our two revolutions simply illustrate the distinctive trajectory of just two of the major trajectories in the Christian constituency of some 1¾ billion people.

It is worth saying again that none of the broad processes that we assemble under the broad theory of secularization aspects of modernity are straightforwardly inevitable. Some, like social differentiation, are very likely to occur, but contingent on an array of supporting or consonant circumstances. In Western Europe the decline of religious practice with the rise of the megacity is widely documented, but new social inventions can counteract, qualify or reverse it given facilitating circumstances. Indeed, at the cutting edge of modernity the megacity may well be complemented by the mega-church, which in the range of functions it includes almost harbingers a return to the medieval Church. Mega-churches are emerging in Latin America as well as in North America (and Korea) and are even to be found in Eastern Europe. Only Western Europe so far lacks them. In any case, such exemplary instances of the modern city as Dallas or Atlanta or Seoul must have something very close to majority practice. The largest church in the world with a membership of over half a million is in the megacity of Seoul.

All highly general processes, including technical rationality itself, need to be analysed as taking this course or that according to the net consequence of other influences. The direction, or rather the directions, of change depend not on prescribed and automatic consequences of this factor or that, but on the circumscriptions flowing from a gestalt of influences. Nor should we assume that when just one of these highly general processes does occur, it will have the consequences normally expected. This book is about a marginality which much sociological theorizing assumes to mean impotence and privatization whereas, in fact, that *all depends* on time and place. In the times and places now to be analysed, marginality has not meant impotence.

Notes

1. Rowan Ireland (1992) *Kingdoms Come: Religion and Politics in Brazil* (Pittsburgh, Pittsburgh University Press)
2. Roger Lancaster (1988) *Thanks to God and the Revolution* (New York, Columbia University Press).
3. José Casanova (1994) *Public Religions in the Modern World* (Chicago, Chicago University Press).

2

Third Person Christianity in the Third World

*

Over the past thirty or so years the religious map of the world has changed dramatically. In the developed West, the liberal religious establishments have seen their constituencies shrink relative to the constituencies of the conservative evangelicals. In what used to be called the Third World, the World Council of Churches' share of the Protestant constituency has dropped, and a protean indigenous Christianity has emerged indifferent to the agenda of the Western theological intelligentsia. Jürgen Moltmann is not regular fare among South African Zionists or the vast crowds of pilgrims attending the Temple of La Luz del Mundo, Guadalajara.

More often than not, this shift is towards a Pentecostal faith in the gifts of the Holy Spirit – healing, speaking in tongues, exorcism, prophecy, holiness. Overall, depending on how you widen or narrow your definitions, perhaps a quarter of a billion persons are involved, making it comparable to the advance of a 'conservative' Islam. But Islam is about reintegrating whole societies behind a single religious law, whereas this 'conservative' Christianity is a fissiparous movement undermining every kind of unifying ideology. You find it all over non-Islamic Africa and even inside the Coptic Church. You find it in South India, South Korea, the Philippines, Singapore, China and the Caribbean (including Cuba). It is, above all, massively present in Latin America; and in Southern and Eastern Europe you can detect the ripples from Sicily to Kiev, with an outer ripple in Tiblisi. Its world-wide reach was illustrated for me when I saw students preaching first in the main square of Santiago, Chile, and very similar students in front of the Hanseatic town hall in Tallinn, Estonia. This is what is meant by globalization.

Though Latin America is so far the most dramatic instance, the pace of change is so fast that even larger numbers could soon emerge elsewhere – for example, in China. Possibly quite soon, the forty million and more evangelicals who make up 10 per cent of the population of Latin America will be matched by a similar number in China, though they would be no more than 3 per cent of the Chinese population. So, by way of introduction, we can take a look at this Chinese evangelical Christianity before turning to other examples in South India, Zimbabwe and Eastern Europe. A few comparisons around the world will show just how typical the case of Latin America is.

Part of Chinese Protestant Christianity has been co-opted by the state and has restricted freedom of operation; but beyond that corral is a burgeoning evangelical Christianity that keeps a low profile and is most often found in 'house churches'. It is local, autonomous and led by lay people, including female evangelists. It is indigenous, and though it adopts some elements of popular culture, they are recoded in a Christian frame. The take-off point for this kind of faith came in the 1970s after the Cultural Revolution managed to disperse religion in all directions through trying finally to eradicate it. Naturally enough, today's believers remain wary of the state and firmly apolitical. It is hardly surprising that the intensity of emotional release in such scattered groupings can sometimes result in sexual scandal, and even in financial scandal. That goes without saying everywhere. For the most part, though, evangelical Christians are viewed as model citizens who work hard, and even manage to contain the notorious tensions of the Chinese family. Just as in Latin America, most Chinese believers have experienced spiritual healing and dramatic conversion. They often speak in tongues, exorcize demons, are urgent in prayer for spiritual goods (and perhaps material goods as well), and they believe God exercises a direct oversight over the details of their daily lives.

Something very similar is happening in southern India. A large proportion of professing Christians in India now belong to activist churches with charismatic leaders. They emphasize the Bible and the gifts of the Spirit, including urgent prayer, exorcism, healing and prophecy. Their churches promote corporate and personal discipline and seek out the presence of the supernatural in everyday life. Each community is built up around individual lay people's assemblies and lay leadership, and members are mostly hostile to established hierarchies. Women find such churches highly attractive, partly because many of them have husbands working away in the Gulf, and partly because they appreciate the opportunities offered to female adepts.

As in Latin America, parallel changes are occurring in the older mainstream churches of India and among middle-class Christians. The Roman Catholic authorities have responded by encouraging an emotional lay piety, including healing. But a major problem for all conventional religious authorities is that they look relativistic, liberal, compromising and weak, especially when faced with militant Hindu communalism and the very concrete powers of non-Christian deities. The big advantage of the new evangelical movements is their defence of a fragile but genuine Christian stake in the social order, a marking out of terrain, and a specifically Indian reclamation of living presences and concrete powers. Some of the organizational models may be picked up from elsewhere, but the dynamism, the personnel and cultural kernel are Indian.[1]

A glance at Pentecostalism in Zimbabwe tells you something of its power to adapt and to run along the lines of fissure in local society. In Zimbabwe, Pentecostalism helps deal with the spiritual aftermath of the guerrilla war and it takes over from the failure of party political and state action. It deals with the really pressing problems of everyday life. Above all, it offers a way forward for aspiring young men and women in their struggle with the patriarchal cults of traditional religion. How many Pentecostals there are in Zimbabwe is difficult to estimate, but one group alone, the Assemblies of God, claims a million members. That means it includes 10 per cent of the population and is the largest church in the country.

The transformation of the spiritual landscape is carried on in various ways, including contests over holy terrain. When it comes to witchcraft, Pentecostals fight fire with fire through exorcism. Women stand to benefit because they suffer most from witchcraft accusations, and if involved in witchcraft themselves they can be exorcized and have recourse to repeated confession and so be restored to full acceptability. Women also benefit because most Pentecostals employ both Western medicine and spiritual healing together, and because they carry out a rigorous attack on beer, tobacco and male rampage. Of course, Pentecostal churches are under male control, and they can gradually revert over time to a Pentecostal version of patriarchy, but the spiritual gifts of prophecy, tongues and healing are still available to all, including young men and women. They can now enjoy access to the most powerful Spirit of all, and if one Pentecostal group rigidifies, then the leadings of the Spirit create another to restore free availability and egalitarian participation.

On the wider political scene, the Pentecostal churches gain because state action is often intrusive, bureaucratic and corrupt, and because the mainstream churches often act as agencies of government action (which may, of course, be much-needed development). Pentecostal churches also play a part in exorcizing guilty consciences and avenging spirits after the atrocities of the guerrilla war, and they retune songs once used for mobilization to the wavelength of spiritual pilgrimage. Songs are very important. As in Latin America, Pentecostalism is only partly an advance of the 'Word'. It is also the advance of the Songs of Zion.[2]

In Eastern and Central Europe, these changes are not so far advanced. In Romania, for example, the 1–2 per cent of the population who have embraced evangelical Christianity hardly compares with the numbers in

Zimbabwe and southern India, let alone China and Latin America. However, things are moving all the same, and Church and state both show signs of alarm. As in Latin America, this form of religion represents the fragmentation of monopolies, both political and religious, thus converts easily find themselves excommunicated as 'not Romanian'. As a matter of fact, evangelical Christianity arrived in Romania over a century ago through the work of German Baptists. But the present upsurge began only in the 1970s during the very dark times of the Ceausescu regime with a spiritual awakening in the frontier city of Oradea. Twenty years later, Oradea has the largest Baptist Church in Europe, holding 3,000. In February 1995 it opened to Handelian Hallelujahs and a British diplomatic presence.

Second Baptist, Oradea, is regularly filled on Sundays and it abuts a Baptist institute of higher education brimming with many hundreds of students. Like the congregation, the students come from both the Hungarian- and Romanian-speaking communities, as well as from Moldova, the Ukraine – and even Siberia – and they are remarkably fluent in English. Perhaps there is some connection between the world-wide spread of English and the world-wide spread of evangelicalism. The master plan of the pastorate and of the Rector Dr Paul Negruţ is to spread out in a star formation and preach the message anywhere from Albania to Russia.

Of course, buildings on this scale do require money from abroad, and it comes mostly from the US, but the spiritual initiative is Romanian. Looking at the assembled congregation in Second Baptist, Oradea, you see a row of faces of people recently arrived in (or driven to) the towns, and then another row of faces of young people ready to take up the professions. You can spot the arrival of the future by listening to the offerings of the musical department under their young American director. The young people in the music department choir not only render evangelical anthems, but can give very respectable accounts of Schütz or Bach, Haydn, Fauré, or Brahms. In them you see the same extending ladder of cultural competence that you find all over Latin America. Reading the Bible leads on to literature in general, sermonizing leads on to argumentation, popular Christian music to Johann Sebastian Bach.

But that is where the danger lies. Aiming to produce articulate Christians can mean some of your best students are drained off into the wider society. Opportunities available in one generation through the pastorate are extended sideways in the next generation by all the chances (and dangers) of higher education. Drain can follow gain, and C.S. Lewis can lead to Les Fleurs du Mal. A student who brought back Derrida from London University was told by one irate listener that he had had enough enforced lack of communication under Ceausescu to put up with the idea that coherent meaning was impossible anyway. At the same time, the intelligence, commitment and energy of these young students put the products of many prestigious Western universities to shame. Not many Western students can take five hours' concentrated lecturing at a stretch.

What you find in Romania, and for that matter in Nigeria, Korea and Brazil, is a subculture that exposes to view potentialities that have been buried for centuries. The volcanic action of evangelical churches throws up underground strata and upends them for the first time to public view. They are now on stage as public actors.

Modern communications help because they make possibilities audible and visible over long distances and to everybody. Evangelical religion has a special affinity with modern technology, because it receives messages and can amplify them. Evangelists enjoy amplification even if some of their neighbours are less well pleased. It comes as no surprise to find a Christian radio station in the offices of the Romanian Missionary Society, Oradea, though it is a bit surprising to find it run by an articulate Pentecostal who knows his way around, intellectually as well as technically. Pentecostals also expand in Romania and today they probably outnumber Baptists two to one. Their style is more direct and popular. Pentecostals are more swayed by the motions of the Spirit than Baptists and less inclined to the expository severities of the Baptist sermon. All the same, they too are exposing a buried intelligentsia to view, and one not yet affected by Western lassitude and relativism.

Pentecostals have substantial communities not only in the pluralistic north-west of Romania, but in Moldavia, where there is apparently a complete Pentecostal village. It seems unlikely, but if you have encountered a Presbyterian village under the hot sun of the Yucatan, you are already prepared to believe it. One Orthodox priest even complained to me of a village with a dangerously critical mass of Jehovah's Witnesses. Evangelical outreach extends further across the Romanian border into Moldova, as well as into the Ukraine, which already counts as a pluralist society. And if there are Witnesses to be complained about, there are also Mormons – though so far only 400 of them in Romania. But they are there, out on the trail, all the way from Utah, along with the Adventists. The New Age is around too, mixed in with reviving recollections of the occult, astrology and items of personal magic. The woman in the train carriage carries an ikon promising safety on her journey and the lorry driver opposite talks of celestial visitors to our planet dimly recorded in the Bible.

One development in Romania that echoes Latin America is the appearance of dedicated youth groups sitting loose to the hierarchies of the established churches, whether Catholic or Orthodox, and sharing – or pre-empting – some of the characteristics of the free-ranging evangelicals and Pentecostals. The Lord's Army within Orthodoxy dates from as far back as the 1920s, and its recent samizdat literature and history of persecution shows how influential it has been. Certainly the Ceausescu government tried to suppress it, maybe with the collusion of some powerful people in the Romanian Orthodox Church. Its membership reaches well into six figures and, like the evangelicals, it encourages lay participation and spiritual gifts. Thousands come to Sibiu for its meetings at Pentecost, and it is today under the impressive leadership of Father Mihoc.

The Lord's Army is unique in Orthodoxy, but even more surprising is a young ginger group in the Hungarian-speaking Reformed Church led by Lazlo Tokes, now Bishop, and previously the pastor who set off the December 1989 revolution. These young people are an intellectual elite fed up with the Loadicean lukewarmness of much of Reformed Christianity. They meet in dedicated cells and hold meetings in the public parks that are very reminiscent of the others I have seen in Tallinn and Santiago. Perhaps this is an echo within Christianity of the intensities that in Islam foregather in the 'wild' mosques and avoid the state sponsored 'big mosques'. Happily, in this Christian version there is little likelihood of violence.

If you cross the border into Hungary, things are less far forward. Somehow one would not expect Hungary to be host to a major incursion of evangelical religion. Budapest in particular is too sleek and sumptuous, with its wide boulevards and Art Nouveau atmosphere. There, expansion of classical Pentecostalism is only modest, but the group that makes the headlines is the 'Faith Church', now accepted as the fourth largest religious group in the country. What this group shows is the ability of a version of charismatic Christianity to adapt to professional middle-class milieux and to operate in the drug culture with a Christian simulacrum of the high-tech vibrant style of the rock concert. The Faith Church is yet another megachurch on the same model you find in Dallas, Texas, or Akron, Ohio, or Atlanta, Georgia, and all over Latin America from Guatemala City to Buenos Aires. Talk to the young religious executives who run the Church, and you find they have an international network of contacts that include Buenos Aires or Sâo Paulo – or Nigeria.

The Faith Church reminds one immediately of the 'Renascer', Church in Sâo Paulo, Brazil, where converts from the drug culture use Christian rock to convert others from the drug culture. Though it attracts people from many social class groups, it clearly includes some from the technological and professional cadres now expanding in Hungary, and also appeals to

some young people from Reformed (Calvinist) families. The Faith Church has – inevitably – been accused
of improprieties, though these are a media stock in
trade. Currently it has plans for its own radio and
television channel. It has well-publicized links with
the government through highly placed members in the
neo-liberal party, and though it has no official political
line, the atmosphere is of the social market. Leaders
describe it as pro-capitalist, though against 'wild' capi-
talism. Not surprisingly, their literature includes many
contemporary authors promoting a 'prosperity gospel', Hagin, Copeland and others. Presumably there is
enough prosperity around in Budapest and enough
hope to make it plausible.

However, there is something else in the Faith Church
that echoes trends in Latin America. It is a hint – no more
– of Christian Zionism, and in Latin America it has been
strong enough for some leaders to be invited to Israel.
It is natural enough in one way, because if groups are
biblically based they are relating to the Hebrew Scrip-
tures: 'They shall prosper that love thee, O Jerusalem'.
The young people of the Faith Church have published
an excellent study of the effects of the holocaust in
Hungary. Looking at this study immediately threw my
mind back to the pictures of the Temple Mount displayed
in the offices of 'Renascer' in Sâo Paulo and to the Meno-
rah which stands prominently in the vast temple of the
'La Luz del Mundo' Church in Guadalajara, Mexico.
Neither this nor the prosperity gospel are central to, or
perhaps even at home in, the universe of classical Pentecostalism represented by the Assemblies of God, but
this strain of theology is plainly evident in the world of
free-floating charismatic enterprise.

A sociological overview

Surveying these movements world-wide shows that they have a close affinity with the movements in Latin America. Though they have long-term historical roots in Anglo-American and Afro-American culture (as well as links in personnel and overlaps in organizational style), they are indigenous religious enterprises based on self-help and mutual aid. Mostly they are concentrated among the respectable poor, but with variant forms in the middle class. Typically they are foremen, artisans, domestic servants, nightwatchmen, small vendors.

Such movements help erode all-embracing systems in politics or in religion and can best be understood through two frameworks. One is Halévy's argument that evangelical conversion assists peaceful cultural evolution rather than violent revolutionary upheaval. The other is De Tocqueville's argument about the way in which voluntary religious organizations build up 'social capital' through networks between the state and the individual. They mostly seek to bypass politics and the state and established religious bodies, and sometimes all three allied together.

Evangelical churches find this comes quite naturally because they go back to bodies like the Methodists, which long ago severed the link between Church and state; but their recent experience of corruption in politics and oppression by the state also helps. They rightly expect very little from corrupt political bureaucracies, or patronage networks, or rival elites in remote political classes. They believe that the only practical and efficient way forward is to create an inviolate social space that they can truly call their own, and where they can with dignity renew themselves. As they go about creating this space they further accelerate the shift to pluralism, because they are so competitive and fissiparous in temper and so anxious to secure local autonomy. They keep themselves alive *and* they pro-create by dividing.

For women, these groups offer a sisterhood of shared experience, and the opportunity for social learning and expression, even though the leaders are generally male. For men they offer an alternative to the macho style, focused on nurture rather than on violence, self-indulgence and sexual rampage. That means they help to bring together the family. Their aim is wholeness of body and spirit achieved by emotional release, and by spiritual healing and Western medicine combined. For the most part, Pentecostals will try anything that works, and what works in their situation is easily experienced as something of a 'miracle'. In their worship they are expressive, participatory and tactile, but in their work ordered, trustworthy and disciplined. Though some of them make syncretic borrowings from time to time, these are usually reworked inside the Christian scheme.

Pentecostals are an option of the poor rather than the liberationist 'option *for* the poor', and this option is most of all exercised by those who seek all-round betterment. In the long run they offer modest social mobility to most, and rapid mobility to a few. Naturally, many people find their beliefs and practices bizarre, but there is little that would have shocked the eighteenth-century Anglo-American evangelist George Whitefield, and rather a lot of that simply comes from taking the New Testament seriously. Another sign of this is their aversion to personal or political violence. Like the Quakers in England in 1661, they are 'the quiet in the land'; but they have also found out how to mobilize the power of marginality and of protective enclosure. They are people who show what can be done by actively attacking your immediate circumstances. They encounter limits, of course, but they also extend them.

Turning to Latin America – the advanced case: a comparison with base communities

One way of opening this up is to compare free-range evangelical and Pentecostal groups in Latin America with the 'base communities'. These are also in their way socially marginal, but they operate from within the Roman Catholic Church and thus are connected to inside resources of intellectual and cultural power. Unfortunately, neither group is correctly portrayed in the Western media. Though evangelicals are probably five times as numerous as those in base communities, they have been virtually ignored till quite recently, or else dismissed slightingly as agents of American imperialism or adjuncts of discredited televangelism. The base communities, on the other hand, have been viewed through the theoretical proposals and rhetoric of liberation theologians, not through observation of their actual operation. So, while Pentecostals and evangelicals have been characterized as introverted salvationists, people in base communities are regarded as dedicated agents of social structural change. But the contrast is not so stark, and some observers are coming to see both groups as intimations of civil society, capable of clearing a space outside the corruptions of the political arena, and a space, moreover, in which people can re-create themselves.[3]

A good example of more recent approaches is provided

by the Marxist anthropologist, Roger Lancaster, in his book on Nicaragua entitled *Thanks to God and the Revolution*.[4] Apparently the evangelical proportion of the population rose from 5 per cent to perhaps 20 per cent during the Sandinista period, and most of all in the poorest barrios of Managua. Lancaster describes the response of the believers as 'creative despair'. They are, he says, typically vendors in the informal economy converted as whole families after some trauma of illness followed by healing. In his view, they present the dynamic alternative to the 'Popular Church', and they attract converts on account of their personal example – *not* on account of manipulative intervention from the USA. Lancaster adds that they do not rob or fight, and are an instalment of orderliness and personal discipline that any government might be disposed to welcome.

How, then, do the base communities resemble Pentecostal churches and how do they differ from them? A local study by William Hewitt of base communities in Brazil puts matters in perspective.[5] The communities resemble Pentecostal churches in being mostly comprised of women; in being for the most part devotional rather than political; in creating a social space for self-governance, social learning, personal leadership, initiative and responsibility; in deploying a language of spiritual power and in railing against the corruption and violence of the powerful; in fighting drugs; in eschewing idolatry and formalism; in putting salvation before religion; in creating a standard and fluent rhetoric of persuasion; and in pursuing holiness.

These are multiple similarities. A further comparison with respect to women is instructive. Both groups empower women, but within the limits set by the culture.

In the base communities women take positions of authority, but largely in versions of their domestic roles. The moment they attempt to organize on their own or to put issues like contraception on the agenda, they are reined in by priest or trade union official or husband. In the Pentecostal churches women run weekday groups, conduct choirs and prophesy, but are rarely allowed to be pastors. Women are channels of devotion and exercise active influence in varied roles but they do not possess the central powers of administrative control. Nevertheless, as Ruth Marshall comments in a sympathetic study of them in Nigeria, born-again men and women do alter their behaviour to each other dramatically, and in particular women receive respect and are delivered from the unequal barter of sexual favours.[6]

How to sum up the differences? First and foremost the leadership of the base communities, whether it be lay person, catechist, priest or whoever, is ultimately under the control of the Catholic hierarchy. Of course, this gives members the visibility, prestige and protection of the Church, and a means of access to the whole society. However, the hierarchy can always withdraw support and in some cases has already done so. By contrast, the Pentecostal pastor more often than not has to keep his head down because his voice would not be heard, and if it were raised too loudly his subsequent disappearance would not be noticed. Another difference is that when base communities from time to time pursue political issues, for example, with regard to local sewerage, paving, lighting, etc., they do so as a matter of theoretical principle, whereas if Pentecostals get involved it is entirely pragmatic. Perhaps the crucial underlying difference is that Pentecostals have dramatically walked out of society in order to construct their own raft, away from the pull of the mainstream and of their own past. It is this resolute stance on the margin and the adamant pursuit of autonomy that feeds on and supports the theological contrast between 'Church' and 'World'. Clearly, they are dualist to a degree that the base communities are not, although I would add that Christianity itself depends for its dynamic on some dichotomy of Church and World.

The difference between Pentecostalist evangelical groups and Catholic associations is perhaps best illustrated from the different consequences for the immediate 'life world' of women. Here we see the advantages enjoyed by women within the non-Catholic groups, and also how these are related to the marked duality of Church and World and the extent of the walk-out from mainstream society. Elizabeth Brusco in her pioneering studies has already drawn attention to the images of nurture appearing in evangelical discourse and to the erosion of the macho model of maleness.[7] More recently, this has been fleshed out by John Burdick in comparisons between the varying situations in which women find themselves in Catholic and evangelical groups.[8] Burdick provides a graphic description of the disaster overtaking the family in the burgeoning megacities of Latin America. There have always been weaknesses in Latin American family structure, but now households are riven apart by a loss of parental control, by profligate male behaviour and expenditure, and by the threat to male prestige created by unemployment. It is here that Pentecostal and evangelical religion enjoys an advantage. In this area, the priest is not necessarily that experienced, and crucially Catholic associations are *tied in* to the neighbourhood with all that that means in terms of gossip and reputation. Of course, the good Catholic woman always has recourse to 'Our Lady help of Christians', but the Blessed Virgin offers her succour to the woman in her loneliness and isolation. As for the prayer specialists and traditional blessers, they have been disastrously downgraded by contemporary Catholicism. From the point of view of Catholic influence in the local population, few policies have been more disastrous than the weakening of the link between women's need and recourse to saints or folk practices.

Of course, Pentecostal believers have themselves rejected recourse to saints, and in theory at least avoid folk practices, but what they offer is renewed sources of immediate power and – in Burdick's view – an opportunity for troubles and afflictions to be talked over beyond the reach of neighbourly gossip, as well as soulful transitions so powerful that many men are reformed and take up their neglected responsibilities. Men do, indeed, recover their fatherly prestige, but only because they now act in a fatherly and responsible manner. The woman now has a framework within which to influence an errant husband, and both of them in alliance can hope to influence their children. Moreover, this domestic reconciliation is made the more easily because the source of evil is not located solely in the self, but in demonic powers that can be defeated. That defeat is only possible, however, provided the Pentecostal community is separated from the wider neighbourhood and its wagging tongues. Thus it can be for entirely local and immediate reasons that a 'walk out,' into principled marginality is necessary and effective.

Latin America : the religious premiss
behind their enterprise

The religious premiss to which evangelicals in Latin America adhere and respond is that human beings universally have 'no power of themselves to help themselves' when it comes to the one thing necessary. The poor, who lack entanglement in the false supports provided by 'the world', are specially open to this truth (just as the gospel itself makes clear), but once it is accepted in the heart with a repudiation of the past, all things become possible in the strength of God. Everything else is 'added to them', which means superabundance of spiritual gifts, but also (as they themselves observe) this often incidentally includes betterment in every sphere, including the material.

These people change themselves or rather seek to be changed, and it is precisely this beginning in the personal sphere, with everything it also means for the reform of the family, as well as for the creation of a new network of relationships, that is so powerful. It means that even from the external observer's standpoint, poor people are able in some degree to change their circumstances. Communities of faith are also communities of hope, and they mobilize ingenious energy that spills over into increased capacity to survive. Again, this is not to say that a community of faith comes into being because it offers a tactic for survival. It is to say that when people seek to rope themselves together on very slippery slopes, maintain disciplines, respect certain priorities, husband the emotional and other capital sunk into their families, and above all have a God-given validation of the value of their own lives and persons, then their life chances are genuinely enhanced.

Lives come to be valued through the experience of being personally delivered in the core of your being, which is what is meant by the familiar phrase about responding to a 'personal Saviour' – a God who is likewise 'personal' and 'in all points as you are'. Evangelical religion provides empowerment through its offer of healing, its demand for responsibility, and its invitation openly to affirm and express. For people to be addressed in evangelical language as persons is to be spoken to in terms that truly speak to their condition, confirming beyond the shadow of doubt their dignity, worth and significance.

Persons are not only affirmed as persons, but called upon to make judgements about themselves and about their own lives. By extension, they are encouraged to make their own judgements in each and every sphere. This is how the unequivocal, authoritative declaration of the preacher becomes the foundation of the autonomy of the hearer. Once that is established as the premiss of your existence, you cannot shuffle everything sideways on to circumstance (the things that 'stand around') or view yourself solely as victim rather than as agent. It is just when your circumstance is most severely limiting and when structures are most obdurately resistant that you need to know yourself as agent, otherwise you will be passively swept over the abyss.

Personal address and the call to a comprehensive betterment must include complete cancellation of all inherited and acquired debts. The phrase 'forgive us our debts' resonates with special power wherever people are enmeshed in every kind of bondage and indebtedness.

If in the past you violated your own self or haplessly co-operated in its violation, you are cut free from that entanglement. And you are set on a narrow path to betterment by being freely accepted by others who also share the goal of improving themselves and their 'lot'.

To most people in the professional and political classes of Western society, a direct address of this kind, person to person, means something rather different to what it means in Latin America or Africa. In the Western middle classes it is resented as an attempt to colonize intimate space with repetitive formulae and banality; but to those who have never heard their name spoken before, it is like the first touch wakening them from centuries-long sleep. They have heard their name 'spoken in the great congregation' and so they repeat those formulae about the receipt of a new Spirit over and over again like besotted lovers to affirm and confirm their happiness.

For such people, the primary need is not to be intrigued, amused or diverted, or even to demonstrate capacity in some respected role. All these things belong to 'the world'. They are 'what the Gentiles seek after', whether it is football, beer, sex or television. The deep need remains to be touched in your heart and to celebrate that touch. The heart, the 'corazon', is now truly established as the seat of all the affections. To be converted there relieves one of the need to be diverted elsewhere. Indeed, it leads to the suspicion that diversion as such is contrary to conversion, and so by another incidental consequence ensures that you are a committed student or a persistent worker. You don't waste your time but, as the seventeenth-century Puritans used to say, you redeem it. You might even end up by being punctual.

The formulae of salvation are biblical, and so Pentecostals and evangelicals speak a 'language of Zion'. This is almost a patois or secret tongue, and it helps seal the group against the outside and reinforces the tendency to introversion. The Bible is of supreme importance partly because it carries awesome authority even in the outside world, and partly because the believers are those who alone have divined its inner meaning and spirit. Other people may have a nodding acquaintance with it, but they are its intimates. They know what it is to have *the* Book in their own hands, not carried in priestly solemnity by someone from whom they are divided by the great gulf of status. What had been an object of deferential genuflection becomes a personal possession, thumbed and worn to shreds by constant pondering. When they defend the Bible it is much less on account of its literal truth and what observers label 'fundamentalism', than because for them it is the bearer of good and perfect gifts.

Believers hold conversations with God and the biblical characters 'as a man speaks to his familiar friend'. The saints vacate their plinths in Baroque space and walk the street as fellow-artisans. And just as 'redeeming the time' might end up in punctuality, so responding to the power of the Word ends up in increasing your word power. The volumes next to the Bible on the shelf are the commentary and the dictionary. The language of Zion is supplemented by a widening vocabulary, some of it archaic and occasionally mispronounced, but perfectly well understood. The cultus broadens out into a culture.[9]

Pastors and lay preachers mostly lack formal training; 'The Lord gave the Word' and a company of preachers sprang up validated by the Spirit. They are, therefore, on the same level as others they meet in their daily life, not distanced by long periods of professional training and learning. The lay missionaries preaching in the street, whether men or women, know the conditions of those they preach to, and take their stories and illustrations from shared experience. So the safe distance acquired through a special language of Zion is relieved by a close proximity in everyday living.

Anyone can aspire to lead and serve, and there is a wide variety of opportunities for leadership and service. This is how those with little or no experience of power in the everyday gain that experience within the evangelical community. Moreover, it is real power, conceded and acclaimed by their equals 'in the Spirit' out of respect for their calling 'in the Lord'. Continual reference to 'the Lord' is not merely pious unction, but a way of claiming the right to speak, or indeed to 'cry out in the street' like some latter-day prophet.

The Latin American pastor speaks 'with authority', partly no doubt because that is the local cultural style, but fundamentally because the right to speak is validated 'by divine permission' and by the shared criteria of the community. This offers a route to a certain amount of abuse because power issuing from the mouth can easily go to the head, and because those who have been subject to the will of others may in turn try to subject others to their will. 'Permission to speak' is bound to be dangerous, even heady. There is a relation between open access to power, radical equality before God, and the dangers of authority. Once you open up leadership in the community to 'unlearned and ignorant men', you have simultaneously increased equality and opened up opportunities for the raw exercise of charismatic potency.

Certainly the Word that such people deliver is no tentative and non-judgemental suggestion. It is exhortation and excoriation. Pastors talk from the heart to the heart, and have no truck with exegetical footnoting. This kind of leadership demands a great deal of personal discipline, and it requires discipline from its hearers to 'bring into subjection' the unruly and wasteful affections of the heart.

Evangelical language, because directed from persons to persons, differs from any political language based on a collectivist rhetoric of the masses or 'the people'. It therefore bypasses politics as the main highway to dignity and worth. Change is not postponed to the Day of the Revolution, but is available here and now. It is political salvation that is perceived as 'pie in the sky'. Above all, religious exhortation is not a call made to collective agents to mobilize 'forces', but a call to personal agents to practise peaceability and acquire a new reformed temper. Peace in the soul goes with peaceability of attitude.

Yet Pentecostalism is political in its indirect consequences and especially because it renders visible persons who were previously invisible. Evangelicals have been socially invisible up to recently, and many of them live in the invisible sectors of the city. Eventually, though, they constitute a presence and attract modest attention. Even to be 'everywhere spoken against' is a form of attention, and it can be handled in a language of suffering readily available from the New Testament: 'Rejoice and be glad when everyone speaks against you'.

At the very same time, evangelicals can also approve of themselves, and feel they are accorded a wider social approval because they are 'labourers worthy of their hire'. The world out there may be bemused by their 'bizarre' practices, but it respects their sobriety and reliability. The mistress of the Catholic household approves of her evangelical domestics because they work by inner conviction and will not invite a male companion in to plunder the household. The owner of the medium-sized business feels the same. Firms beyond a dozen or so workers depend on trust, conscience and conscientiousness.

The sense of self-worth, partly validated by the contemptuous world itself, builds up into a certain pride in what has been achieved, and this can eventually lead to self-advertisement and unctuous righteousness. Since the seventeenth century, Protestant piety has attracted satire on this account all the way from Ben Jonson in *The Alchemist* to George Eliot and Anthony Trollope. But it is very understandable that those who live out their lives in narrow rooms look round their church and feel that this is something they have created and can be proud of. They gave the donations or tithed, or even helped in the building itself. A woman looking round at the assembled faces of her sisters, many of whom were once abandoned or abused, feels that this is redemption not only from hell, but from a social abyss. The pastor who dug the ditches for the lavatories with his own hands knows that this is the Lord's doing – and his own.

The community, through its physical church and in the raising of its voice through hymns and spiritual songs, announces it is there. A first and crucial step has been made towards secure social and personal being and it is bodied forth in the murmurous power of prayer or in shouts of acclamation. Large numbers gather symbolically 'at the river' and carry each other 'over Jordan', and then sing into the early hours of their deliverance and of what has been accomplished. It is this passive tense of what has *been* done on one's behalf that confirms your inner security more than anything one might claim for oneself. Evangelicalism is spoken in the passionate personal passive.

It follows that wearing your best clothes to church is an act of respect for what has been granted rather than a claim to status. Of course, eventually the two elements of gratitude to God and of respectability in the eyes of others may switch places so that the suit is indeed a social and personal claim. At that point, social exclusion can take over from social inclusion and the poorer brethren begin to feel 'out of place'. But that possibility is already allowed for in the controls exercised over ostentation. Eventually those who find the controls irksome slip away to some other church that is more 'advanced', more relaxed, and perhaps more culturally up-market.

Most Pentecostals, however, have come in from the margins and now know themselves to stand on the right side of a line approved by God – not by society. They were first of all 'put right' by God *alone* and they literally feel (and are) 'good' as they stand respectable and decently suited outside their chapel at the end of the service and shake the pastor's hand. This is the chatter and banter of those who have crossed from death to life. Their brushed and shining exteriors show that they have made the great transition. Unless one understands the way that divine validation literally and psychically turns people around, you cannot understand what is going on at all.

This transition is a drama in which you are a participant actor, and you are encouraged to come centre stage and tell your story about how the transition was made. The pastor's sermon mirrors and supports your story, mixing it with homely jokes and simple pathos, and adding encouragement and admonition. The most powerful drama of all comes with the really big meeting because in that your story is confirmed as Grand Narrative. The truth is now publicly validated in the great assembly and those little people who don't count in their ones and twos can at least count as 'the great multitude which no man can number'. (In one sense numbers matter enormously and are clearly part of the claims of Catholicism itself. On the other hand, there is the counter-claim that 'Where two or three are gathered together there am I in the midst'.) You are the suffering ones and you are the triumphant ones. One way or the other you will win through.

The pastorate: a buried intelligentsia

The best vantage point for appreciating the strengths and weaknesses, achievements and blunders of Pentecostalism and conservative evangelicalism is in the pastorates and the lay leadership. This is where the 'buried intelligentsia' shows its public face. Some of them are ('in their generation') real renaissance men. You need to call up on your mental screen the figure of a canny 5-foot preacher in rural Chile, with the features of the Aymara people and a face as lined as a river bed at low tide. He has been a flyweight boxer and left-wing political organizer. Now he is architect, builder, acupuncturist, journalist, broadcaster and choir master. To teach his children's choir, he has worked out the language of music on his own by moving up and down the staves from middle C. He knows exactly when and where to help miracles happen, and where to find them falling off lorries. This is the kind of man you are dealing with, and he tells you he has outfaced a lion in the Andes in the power of the Lord, just like little David, the Shepherd-King. He is not one to concede advantages to his opponents. As he commented about his old boxing days, 'Did not the Lord say "It is better to give than to receive"?'

You can see such people all over the expanding evangelical world, often burly, square jawed and beetle-browed. They are God's salesmen with noses to the grindstone, exuding an Edwardian confidence and assurance, because they know they have made everything they have – and that God has 'made' them. *They* are the God-made men. Why should they apologize to *you* for such goods as they have? The Good Book says that the Lord will bless the works of their hands, and the evidence is all around them. This is palpable proof (if that is what you want); and if through life's malign chances you go down, you will be borne up with the wings of eagles before you enter the abyss. Did not David say we shall not beg for bread? The circular logic cannot be broken.

The big opportunities and the large temptations for the leadership lie in the mainstream bodies and the mega-churches as they ferry their people in the direction of security and respectability. The myriads of street preachers and pastors in tiny chapels are not likely to be led into temptation in this particular way. To them, Providence has given a tiny edge in the struggle for survival or consolation in acute distress. Among them, the struggle for power and resources is not likely to be morally debilitating and the sins are bound to be minor. Their minute fissiparousness is actually an adaptive advantage in the expansion of the faith, but struggles on the larger scale can encourage larger improprieties and bring about genuinely damaging splits. The stakes matter and in a vast and complex organization like the Assemblies of God in Brazil, major splits really are seriously counter-productive.

Whatever the temptations of success, the local captains of evangelical industry are impressive and ready to engage the wider world. They are brokers for the body of the faithful. As one pastor who had founded over a hundred churches put it to me: 'I'm studying law in my sixties because I need to know how to cope with the local administration'.

Another pastor I met ran housing collectives and classes in business administration for his people, and had the ear of the Governor to help him build a mega-church on a prime site. He had taken very seriously the Gospels' advice to be as wily as a serpent as well as in-nocent as a dove. Holy idiocy is not a stance admired by such people. Knowing how to build, he had built his own house. There it was, complete with double garage and discreetly shielded by railings and trees. Inside, the interior gleamed opulently on split levels, decorated with photographs of strapping sons and daughters, as well as with balloons and enormous cuddly bears. The pastor's wife presided in matronly efficiency, a domestic moved quietly about, and the pastor sank into his chair to declare that the Lord has been good. For such a man, what scope could be offered him as an anonymous follower in the vast crowds following the statue of our Lady into a gold-encrusted shrine?

He is an exception, but his more modest peers are also

practical men validated by their passionate addiction to work. One interviewed me (rather than the other way round) and illustrated nearly every proposition in Max Weber's 'Protestant Ethic' in two hours' unstoppable exposition. It was time, he said, that the Hispanic world showed the energy of the Japanese, the Germans and the Americans. His social work was to help ensure that social workers had no clients who needed help. He had applied to Rockefeller to help establish a technological institution. If you wanted humanist education, that was available at the Pontifical University: 'I want skills for my people'. The books on his shelves told the same story; they were the tools for the job.

Most of the churches served by this pastorate are utilitarian and plain, though with pleasing bright colours and an iconography of still waters and of roses of Sharon and lilies of the valley. But, again, successful ministers can be led into the temptations of giantism and future debt. They may prefer the glory of Solomon to the lilies of the field. The man who 'labours abundantly in the Lord' can be driven as hard as the architects of Beauvais or the megalomaniac Dean in William Golding's *The Spire*. 'I fear we may have entered our cathedral phase', mused one pastor to me, a scholar-missionary from the Canadian Maritimes with a PhD from Aberdeen. Neither of us smiled when I said I needed to look up the Cappadocian Fathers, and he replied that the complete Migne's *Patrologiae* was there in the library. Pastors certainly see the humanist arts as Laodicean diversions, but there is a strain in contemporary evangelicalism that is almost rabbinic in its application to 'the law of the Lord'.

So while there are the hedge preachers and street

vendors in one part of the Vineyard, there are articulate, highly trained people in another. One I met in the USA was a highly qualified female pastor, slightly disabled, who was leaving the Pentecostals not because she had lost faith, but because her church was not using her to the full. There, too, lies another avenue of loss, because there is a buried intelligentsia of women as well as of men coming out into the open air through these churches. At some point their wealth of early opportunity becomes an impoverishing constriction. After all, this is, in a sense, a women's movement, in tune with the undercurrent of Christianity throughout its history from the discovery of the three Marys in the Easter garden right up to today.

What these examples from the buried intelligentsia illustrate is the wide range of Pentecostal and conservative evangelical advance. The mainstream versions are in the classical Pentecostal tradition represented by a large church like the Assemblies of God in Brazil or the Methodist Pentecostal Church in Chile. But apart from these giants there are myriads of tiny groups, some no more than a single home or a shack attached to a home in a poor suburb. The suburb of La Pintana in Santiago is honeycombed with these, and so are the hills above the road snaking past Tijuana in Baja California. They are built by the very poor for themselves and for whoever will join with them. They have titles like 'Voice in the Desert' or 'Prince of Peace'. Inside them, the pastor-husband speaks in the evening from a makeshift podium only a few feet from their chicken run, while his wife maybe preaches in the street when the children emerge from school.

The buried intelligentsia has also created and fostered somewhat syncretic 'deviations' like the 'Universal

Church of the Kingdom of God' in Brazil or 'The Light of the World' in Mexico. Both have a million or two adherents, with branches in the USA, and seem to have a special appeal to non-Hispanic peoples. The Universal Church takes over or erects cinema-like structures opening on to the street and offers exorcism or healings nightly. 'The Light of the World', dating from the interwar period, has created a temple area around a fantastic temple holding thousands in Guadalajara, which is partly New Jerusalem on earth and partly a kind of Ethiopian and Judaic reworking of themes from buried layers of the Mexican psyche. It has many outposts in the USA, and people stream back in pilgrimage to the Mexican temple just as Mormons stream in the other direction to their temple in Utah.

Finally, there are the megachurches with their all-inclusive facilities, their ministerial management teams, their sometimes professional clientele, and their excursions into Christian rock and against the drug culture. And there are the basements and enlarged living rooms of professional homes where the social worker bends over the guitar and the engineer expounds the Word. The variety is almost infinite, but the messages retain their family likeness.

The politics of evangelicalism: covert and overt

We come finally to the issue of the political impact of conservative evangelical Christianity, initially with regard to the covert implications of the forms it takes and then with regard to overt political participation. Perhaps the first point to be made concerns the difference between moral conservatism and a neo-liberal approach to issues of welfare. The former need not imply the latter. The second point concerns the difference in approach that may exist between ordinary congregation and the Pastorate. In so far as pastors have to protect their tenuous institutional stake in times of crisis they may well make short-term political alliances that they later come to regret, and that in the long term bring them into disrepute.

For people far below the level of the political classes, politics is an implicit activity carried on by cultural reorganization. In that sense, it is a political act simply to create a layer of institutions that could be integrated into an emerging civil society. Likewise, it is a political act to establish a free space and to create models of self-government and participation with a flat hierarchy of management.

At a rather different level, conservative evangelicalism in Latin America pursues an implicit cultural politics because it is dedicated both to personal and social peaceability. The taming of the macho personality is all of a piece with the rejection of the romanticism of violence and the role of the guerrilla. It is also all of a piece with the setting-up of an enclave at the social margin that rejects any collusion of Church and state. Conservative evangelicalism has very restricted ambitions with regard to the state, and it has no theory of forcible change designed to overthrow state structures. It desires in every sense to live and let live, so it can only advance by the peaceable slow stain of cultural implication, and even then not by direct intention but through the outworking of the incidental consequences of disciplined faith.

The free space of evangelical activity may pick up and

express many different kinds of previous social alignment that it then remoulds in its own image. For example,
free space may appeal to many of those most exposed
to capitalistic social relations and accelerate that exposure
or, alternatively, it may take many most threatened by
the advent of such relations and throw around them a
protective cordon. Again it may assist local workers in
defending themselves against exploitative middlemen, or
alternatively bolster the ambitions of those who act as
negotiators and brokers between the locality and the
wider world. Where the social world is heaving and
cracking with seismic fissures the lava of faith travels in
many directions, helping redistribute a new landscape
and adapting to a multiplicity of niches. Sometimes it
happens that local society is threatened by new and more
widely based relationships. This can lead to a siphon-
ing off of local power and the Catholic Church may be
identified as complicit in that loss; in that case, free
evangelical space coalesces with a defensive local solidarity. But then the roles can be reversed. Where there are
two (or more) players, and where religion has become
competitive, the rival groups play different roles according to context, and adopt varied guises.

The logic of setting up some enclave of protected free
space on the margin is that evangelicals should sever the
immemorial bonds tying them into local hierarchies and
cut the lateral bonds linking them up with the neighbourhood and its norms of behaviour. These norms may
include corruption, clientship, violence, the abuse and
abandonment of women, the neglect of nurture and
discipline, and the dissipation of resources – especially
on alcohol. The ties most likely to link evangelicals to
this world are those of the fiesta and godparenthood.

Since evangelicals seek 'new life', they have to break with both the fiesta and godparenthood.

By contrast, the Catholic Church must, in accord with its nature and history, remain intimately bound up in such ties, and in so far as power in the society is mediated through successive levels, the Church mimics these levels and parallels them through its own levels of spiritual mediation. This is the case whether or not the Catholic church is critical of social arrangements. What evangelical religion achieves by its very existence is a fundamental tear in the fabric of mediation. They have laid the axe to a major sector of mediated power in the sphere of religion and that has implications for the other spheres. It would not be the first time that mediation is first of all undermined in the symbols and practices of faith, and then undermined across the board. Religious liberty is 'the first liberty' in more senses than one.

The wider theoretical context of all such processes is social differentiation in that in this way and that variegated social spaces are being opened up with their own appropriate autonomy, and the Catholic Church is gradually being prised away from the centripetal hubs of power. Evangelical religion in Latin America is a replication (rather than a diffusion) of differentiations long ago achieved in Anglo-American society, whereby religion does not *have* to be political (i.e. at the core of the polis), but can exercise its influence through culture, including the cultural margin. Morally, evangelicals may be conservative, but sociologically, they are one of the forward sectors of radical social change – above all, because they help along the fragmentation of an inclusive religious hegemony. This further implies that they themselves will not seek, as would 'fundamentalist'

Muslims, to replace one hegemony with another. There never will come a time when the evangelical government of (say) Ecuador imposes the regulations of Deuteronomy on the whole society and abolishes the fiesta and Mardi Gras.

So far as any explicit political alignments of evangelicals are concerned, these are quite varied, though concentrated in the centre and centre-right. Clearly their whole ethos makes it unlikely that they will ally themselves with Marxist or Catholic parties or some combination of the two. There are, however, avenues through which evangelicals can insert themselves in political life short of Catholicism and Marxism. They have now entered national politics in Colombia pressing for equal rights, and they were a significant force in the initial stages of 'Cambio 90', which brought Fujimori to power in Peru. Investigation in Chile and El Salvador suggests that the voting habits of conservative evangelicals are not so very different from their immediate social peers. In certain countries they remain very apprehensive about any kind of participation because of the violence wreaked on them in the past – for example, in El Salvador in the 1930s.

The only countries where evangelicals have entered national politics on a largish scale are Brazil and Guatemala. With regard to the election of Collor as President of Brazil and the defeat of the left-wing candidate Lula, their vote may well have been quite influential. They were naively impressed by Collor's attacks on corruption and afraid of the advance of militant secularism, and may have voted against Lula in the ratio 70:30. Thereafter, they undoubtedly experienced considerable disillusionment on account of

Collor's behaviour in office. Unhappily there was also some disillusionment over the behaviour of some of the evangelical deputies, and at the most recent election in 1994 their representation dropped somewhat.[10] It seems that their fear of corruption and of being drawn into it is well placed.

The response of the mainstream

Where, then, does this leave the mainstream Christian bodies, especially the Catholic Church? The quick answer is: alarmed. The special situation in Latin America has set alarm bells ringing in the episcopal conferences of the continent and in the Vatican itself. In the role of observers and consultants, my wife and I attended a conference in New York between evangelical representatives and members of the Catholic hierarchy in the USA, designed to arrive at 'rules of engagement' between the two most expansive forms of contemporary Christianity.

The argument just made is designed to show why this kind of religion appeals and makes such an extraordinary impact in today's world. No doubt I have brought out the positive side, given that there is no shortage of detractors. Where, though, does this leave the Catholic Church with its constituency of virtually a billion persons and its dominant position in dozens of countries? Clearly, in so far as all kinds of hegemony and authority, whether religious or political, are under threat (and not only from Pentecostalism), it leaves Catholicism shaken. But a tree does not fall because it bends. For one thing, it is possible for Catholicism and evangelicalism to expand together, as they are said to do in Cuba and Guatemala.

The huge new basilica built between Sâo Paulo and Rio with its Bernini-like embrace of all the world hardly symbolizes a Church that has lost its way and its confidence. For another, there are parts of the world, such as Central Africa and Korea, where Catholicism makes rapid progress. It is a truism that vast counter-movements like the Reformation expanded rapidly and then reached a plateau before receding. You have only to look at the forlorn chapels of Bethesda or Bethania in North Wales to read that lesson. Contemporary evangelicalism has not yet reached a plateau, but there is quite a lot of evidence of a revolving door whereby many who enter also soon come out again. The Parable of the Sower applies sociologically.

There are two considerations worth remembering. First, much of what is found in Pentecostalism also exists in Catholicism. Recourse to healing is only one example. Concrete powers also existed in Catholicism had they not been downgraded by the pale cast of abstraction. A quite different example is provided by a reading of *Rerum Novarum*, the papal encyclical of 1891. The economic ethos recommended there sounds startlingly like what is practised among today's evangelicals. Again, when the Chilean bishops recently expressed their anxiety about 'moral anarchy', the people most inclined to share their concerns were the Pentecostals, followed next by practising Catholics.

As the evidence abundantly suggests, vast movements outside the established churches are echoed inside them, and also emulated by those churches in order to remain competitive. To listen to a young Catholic evangelist of 'New Evangelisation 2000' is to hear a vocabulary and an experience virtually identical to that of Pentecostals (apart from references to the Pope and the Blessed Virgin). It is not at all likely that Catholicism will incorporate 'Pentecost' all along the line, but it will and does include it. If the Coptic Church of Egypt can do it, then certainly the Catholic Church can. For that matter, the Anglican Church in Chile undergoes a lively expansion, in part because it too includes a charismatic emphasis. Just as eighteenth-century evangelicalism and later revivalism have fed personnel back over generations into the established bodies, so the same process could be gone through again. If you pursue the genealogies of Anglican hierarchs, they often lead back to enthusiastic lay dissenters who were (maybe) part of some English (or Welsh) 'buried intelligentsia'. The same may be true of the future hierarchs of Roman Catholicism.

Perhaps a future archbishop of Jalisco, Mexico, flourishing *c.* AD 2070, will, instead of anathematizing Protestantism as the third party in a malign Trinity along with drugs and pornography, reminisce fondly about the sterling qualities of his Pentecostal grandparents.

Notes

1. I rely here on the work of Susan Bayly and personal informants.
2. I rely here on the researches of David Maxwell.
3. Daniel Levine (1991) *Popular Voices in Latin American Catholicism* (Princeton, Princeton University Press).
4. Roger Lancaster (1988) *Thanks to God and the Revolution* (New York, Columbia University Press).
5. William Hewitt (1991) *Base Christian Communities and Social Change in Brazil* (Lincoln, University of Nebraska Press).
6. Ruth Marshall (1991) 'Power in the Name of Jesus', *Review of African Political Economy*, 52, pp. 21–37.
7. Elizabeth Brusco (1986) 'The Household Basis of Evangelical

Religion and the Reformation of Machismo in Colombia' (PhD CUNY, Ann Arbor, University of Michigan Microfilms).

8. John Burdick (1990) 'Gossip and Secrecy : Women's Articulation of Domestic Conflict in Three Religions of Urban Brazil', *Sociological Analysis*, 51:2, pp.153–70.

9. Carmen Galilea and Renato Poblete (1984) *Movimiento Pentecostal e Iglesia Catolica en medios populares* (Santiago, Centro Bellarmino).

10. Paul Freston (1993) 'Protestantes e Politica no Brasil' (PhD, Campinas University, SP). For the numerous complexities of the situation of Paul Freston (1996) 'The Protestant Eruption into Modern Brazilian Politics', *Journal of Contemporary Religion*, 11:2, pp.147–68.

3

Eastern Europe: the margin that took centre stage

*

One of the main themes of these three chapters is how those things and those processes that lie at the social margin can, nevertheless, be powerful sources of change. In the case of Pentecostalism in Latin America, I tried to show how poor and marginal people could initiate a revision of consciousness amounting to a cultural revolution. This revolution takes place in a social space that they have devised for themselves as a carefully bounded and protected enclave against the corruptions of the outside world. In the case of religion in Eastern Europe, I want to show how a church, banished to the margin and officially confined to a restricted social space, could become a major conduit of symbolic opposition and, eventually, a major channel of revolution once sufficient co-operating circumstances were present. Nor is this some quirky judgement of a person who has no particular expertise in the politics and culture of Central and Eastern Europe. Timothy Garton Ash has pointed to the resistance of Poland and of the Polish Church as a central key to half a century of struggle.

Of course, the chief modus operandi of faith is by signs and coded signals, whether we are thinking of Pentecostalism in Latin America or the Roman Catholic Church and Orthodoxy in Eastern Europe. But signs and signals are not the hapless emissions of helpless spirits or 'mere' symbolism. Signs denote presences and give notice of an autonomous citadel of the spirit. In Eastern Europe, signs create a bridge to the real presences of remembered past and the ghostly presences of possible future. A signal raises up and resurrects an alternative kind of being in the present. All the churches had to do in Eastern Europe was to continue to be. Some of them had been able to do little else for centuries, but once confronted by a theory that promised their final death and burial by 'the forces of history', their mere being acquired a new and precious significance. Marxist government actually threw into relief what a religious act was and infused the sign with its aboriginal life. It also turned mere survival into a triumph and mere symbolism into open rebellion. The ordinary dubieties of faith were converted into an apodictic affirmation of a transcendent principle beyond the power that comes from the mouth of the gun. It takes two sides to determine the meaning of a sign, just as it takes two to tango.

At this point one needs to recollect the standard problematic of secularization. Secularization is perhaps best understood (and most persuasively documented) as the fragmentation of the comprehensive frames that in the past held together the social world. Things really do fall apart and the centre does not hold, religiously or ideologically. The common religious element collapses, in the polity, in the polis and in the local community. That happens in very different ways, in Latin America, in North America, Western Europe and Eastern Europe. These different ways require brief delineation.

In Latin America, the all-inclusive frame of institutional Catholicism is collapsing and there is now an open market of faiths on which Pentecostalism is a potent competitor. Even in Colombia it is impossible to say that a Colombian is a Catholic. Nevertheless, the collapse of the institutional frame has *not* meant a collapse of the spiritual premiss and a secularization of consciousness. In North America, by contrast, the institutional frame was never securely established, and faith has been offered on a wider and wider open market, but ever since the dawning of modernity that has involved a strengthening of religious institutions, and not a weakening. In Western Europe, the collapse of inclusive religious institutions has occurred more or less quietly in Protestant societies, and with intermittent convulsions in Catholic societies, but in every case secular elites have grasped the heights of symbolic power and have helped reduce the resources of religious reproduction. Religion appears to be part of the external established façade, as in England, but it is implicated in all the contemporary fragmentations. Much of the unifying spirit of the whole has fled, though by no means all.

In Eastern Europe, however, the overprinting of Marxism and communist ideology in 1917, and then again in the late 1940s, brought about something significantly different. This overprinting, and the banishment of religion to the private sphere that followed, reversed roles between religion and secular ideology. Instead of religion being part of the established façade, and being implicated in the fragmentation of the inclusive frame, ideology took its place and suffered the same fate. Communism, by its unabashed and confident occupation of the command-ing heights of public symbolism, and by its claims to a monopoly of truth and power, offered itself to the cor-rosions of the centre. It also offered to religion the happy burden of truthfulness, of martyrdom, of opposition, of alternative ways of being and seeing, of symbolizing things that 'were not' – and, above all, of combining past with future against an oppressive and lifeless present. It divested faith of alienation and invested it with real life, thus simultaneously confirming and disconfirming its own theory. It confirmed its own theory because it defines religion as 'the heart of a heartless world', but disconfirms its own theory in that its own 'leap into freedom' was a leap into despotism, making religion not a false heart but a true one,

There are other elements that mark out Eastern Europe, as well as this overprinting of Marxist ideol-ogy and this reversal of roles. I have argued that the course and fortunes of religion in Latin America and Eastern Europe (as well as, of course, its fortunes in North America and Western Europe) turn to an impor-tant extent on the varied outcomes of the struggle of the Church with radical and enlightened secular elites. I think that is true, and can be seen clearly in places like Uruguay where the radical elites won, in Colombia where they lost, in North America where neither they nor the clergy could find a commanding height to command, and in England where they edged the clergy into a subordinate and debilitating role within the establishment. Nevertheless, in Eastern Europe the radical elites of the classical Enlightenment either did not gain control, or else they manipulated religion as part of a regime of enlightened absolutism. Josephism in Austro-Hungary and the enlightened reforms of Peter the Great secured religion fast within the state, without attacking it among the people at large. This can be put another way. Western competitive democracy came late to Eastern Europe and remained weak, and religion was neither weakened nor free. Religion simply existed as a part of everyday life under authoritarian and mostly imperial regimes: Austria-Hungary, the Ottoman Empire, the Muscovite empire. The only places where enlightened elites held any sort of sway were not really in Eastern Europe at all. They were rather in Central Europe, in Germany for a while before 1933, and in Moravia and Bohemia for a period up to 1938.

For the rest of Eastern Europe, the incursions of enlightened elites had much less thrust and historical depth. Much more likely was some variety of populist or monarchical or clerical semi-Fascism, intermixed with romantic nationalism. At different times and in varied circumstances, regimes of this kind – authoritarian if not exactly Fascist – exercised power in Croatia, Slovakia, Bulgaria and Romania, even maybe in inter-war Poland. In pre-communist Hungary, priests were key political figures. In other words, populations that had experienced only weak and intermittent democracy and were mostly steeped in an everyday folk religiosity, were shifted arbitrarily from the domination of one type of elite, often with strong clerical and monarchical elements, to the domination of an elite claiming to represent radical secular Enlightenment. After all, that identification with the Enlightenment is what Marxism adamantly claims.

What, then, is important in the Eastern European world of today is the partial decomposition of dominant elites as such. As I have already suggested, the ousting of the older elites, clergy included, fast-forwarded social change, leaving the new elites to face the process of decomposition. In some instances that decomposition has been primarily ideological, leaving the apparatchiks of communism as opportunist power holders or power seekers.

This leads to a variety of analyses country by country: the older layer of clerically influenced elites sought a return in Poland riding on the back of populism; in Serbia, Slovakia, Romania and Bulgaria, the sometime communist elites are hiding in wider coalitions with new names, and with less authoritarian methods, in order to retain access to power; in Czechoslovakia, the liberal elites plus some representatives of Christianity sought, at least in the initial stages, to form a common front born of their common suffering; and in Hungary, a segment of the older kind of elite is in confrontation with a radical secular elite in which technocratic and humanist elements are more important than the Marxist rump. All this, it had better be said, is sociological imagination operating at a distance. I can only present conjectures for refutation.

One other element has to be noticed, and it follows from what was earlier said about religion as part of the habitual round of everyday life in much of Eastern Europe. The extent of the habit varies, of course, and it is relatively weak in Serbia, Albania, Montenegro and Bulgaria. In this southern rim there is a kind of passive

Eastern Orthodoxy, mixed in places with Islam. However, it gives rise to an identity of religion and ethnicity increasing in intensity as you go south and east. Poland is the pre-eminent case, but one thinks also of Lithuania, Croatia and Slovakia. Religion is a potent source of union for the people concerned, and so a terrible source of discord between them and their neighbours, especially where ethnic minorities are jumbled together, as in parts of Bulgaria and Romania, in Georgia, Armenia and the Baltic Republics, and in parts of former Yugoslavia. This means that the effect of religion in these areas will be many headed: partly it will be carrying the impulses of continuity, democracy and self-determination, partly undissolved fragments of older mentalities, including ecclesiastical triumphalism, partly the obdurate rivalry between peoples. Above all, that obdurate rivalry has been the case in former Yugoslavia, and the explosive mixture of religion, ethnicity and politics there is already too familiar. In such conditions, what had been the passive religiosity of Serbia gains in self-consciousness, even militancy. In this context there may be some revival of anti-semitism, though of course most of the Jewish communities were either drastically reduced by murder or have emigrated to Israel and elsewhere.

This union of ethnicity and faith will be at its most potent at the major fault lines where the tectonic plates of world religions press into and under each other. What we see in Northern Ireland could be reproduced with far greater intensity where Islam and Christianity meet in Northern Albania, Bosnia and Kosovo, in the Muslim areas of Bulgaria, and in the Caucasus, and it could recur at the borders of Orthodoxy and Catholicism in the western Ukraine and Romania.

This is not a danger confined to Eastern Europe. At the same time, as fragmentation occurs, as the centre loses sway, and as cultural pluralism is acknowledged and even fostered, there is a move towards ethnic and religious homogeneity almost everywhere south-east of Bratislava. Just as the Christian and Jewish populations that once lived with their Islamic neighbours all over the Middle East and North Africa are being squeezed out, so the same process occurs in Russia as the Russians move back to their 'own' Republic; as Georgians and the peoples of the Baltic Republics encounter their own minorities; as Catholics in northern Albania and Muslims in southern Yugoslavia seek to find where they belong or are told where they are to go. Ethnic 'cleansing' is a very old story indeed, as is ethnic 'resettlement'. The Croatian government expels the Serbs from Krajina, and the Serbian government resettles them around Kosovo.

This mosaic of ethnicity and habitual faith points up once again the difference between truly Eastern Europe and what is more properly Central Europe. In Moravia, Bohemia and in eastern Germany you have semisecularized peoples for whom the Church is not 'natural', collective and inevitable, but chosen and individual. But there is another difference. The Catholic Church carries within it Western traditions that give it a political edge, a distinctive autonomous presence in the polity, and a social agenda, lacking in Byzantine Christianity. In Croatia, Poland and Lithuania this brings into being Catholic intelligentsias that have helped to maintain the cultural continuity of their countries. It has also given rise to adamantine ecclesiastics, ambiguously straddling the old theocratic ambition and the proper freedom of the spiritual arm, who became martyrs in Yugoslavia and Hungary, and today excite admiration and/or controversy as saints or as reactionaries (or both!) according to your viewpoint.

In Poland there has always been a rather special situation. The Roman Catholic Church has for so long doubled for the nation, and dealt so successfully and subtly with the communist occupation, that some ecclesiastics could imagine a full-scale restoration in which (as Walesa put it) to be Polish is to be Catholic, where Church and state are once more quarrelling consorts, and where ecclesiastical rules about abortion influence secular law. The role of the present Pope in Polish resistances shored up recent ecclesiastical ambitions. It is quite clear, however, that this is not what most of the 38 million people of Poland want. For example, 60 per cent declared themselves against outlawing all abortion. The Church as sign and rallying point is one thing, but the Church as theocracy is something quite other. In Poland you had, after all, the curious phenomenon of those who were 'pratiquant, non-croyant'. Such persons certainly do not want what some contemporary anti-clericals and some old-style communists call 'Iranization'. The situation probably presages a tension over religious education in state schools which will really be about the control of the power of religious reproduction and the acceptable face of the dominant religion in the public realm.

Yet the main drift of the present argument has concerned the *de*composition of monopolies and establishments, religious and secular, rather than *re*composition. That is going forward in a number of ways that bear on the way the revolutions of 1989 came about. The first has to do with a development visible all along the marches of Central Europe and the West, which is the emergence of small cells and groups partly detached from religious authority. It happened in East Germany, Hungary and western Czechoslovakia. In East Germany, that was not particularly problematic for the Church, since the hierarchy of a Protestant denomination in a secularized society is not all that powerful anyway. In western Czechoslovakia, the emergence of such groups provided an index of the stifling degree of governmental control over the Church, and in Hungary it signalled a rejection of the compromises that the official Church made in order to survive. This rejection actually provided the Church with a lever in its negotiations with the communist state and was at its most intense over peace issues. Indeed, in this whole sector of independent life, surfacing in small groups – above all in East Germany – young people were particularly attracted by the causes of peace and the protection of the environment. They wanted peace and love, not class warfare, the inculcation of hatred, and the imposition of Marxist militarism. In short, some of the 'green' grass that in the West mainly emerged outside the established religious bodies grew up in the East in the sheltered plot provided by the Church.

The second element of decomposition has to do with the emergence of evangelical and Pentecostal groups. That was, of course, central to the decomposition in Latin America, but there are numerous evangelical groups in Poland, and the growth of Baptist and Pentecostal churches in Romania has been quite rapid since the mid-1970s. In Hungary, a 'Faith' Church is now the fourth largest religious group in the country and has links with members of the government and neo-liberal opinion. Much of this growth is indigenous and can sometimes claim longish historical roots, but American religious entrepreneurs of various kinds are also active in promoting their own versions of pluralism. This arouses opposition in many parts of Eastern Europe which, from time to time, includes an alliance of communist, ecclesiastical and liberal nationalists.

The third element concerns decomposition in Russia itself. The dogmatic confidence of the communist system, together with its secure imperial presumption, went into a decline that was probably terminal. Nobody believed any more. Today's Russians look like Westerners and talk like Westerners, and Gorbachev was simply the first and very modest wave of their advent. Yet he made a major difference; it was his decision not to send in tanks, his recognition of the successful obduracy of Poland, his deployment of the KGB against hardline regimes in the GDR, Romania and Czechoslovakia, that were prerequisites of successful revolution. All that, plus the abject economic failure of the whole Soviet project, brought the house of cards down. Of course, what will happen with a resurgent National Communism nobody knows.

The covert sign language of faith and ethnic tradition worked in conjunction with the economic failure and the ideological and moral decay to bring about the overthrow of the system. Indeed, when the conditions were ripe, the sign language of religion shifted from covert to overt, and people began very cautiously to speak in their own voice. In Poland, of course, the signs had always been clear, though made with politic caution. Poland was itself the luminous sign that the system had no root; but elsewhere the signs had been covered over, swathed as if in continuous Lenten season. It is no wonder then that even in Bulgaria, as the coverings were removed, one of the representatives of change spoke of a 'new Easter' in his country, or that the demonstrations in Sofia were accompanied by mass baptisms of adults.

Before looking at the revolutions in different countries it is worth noticing the kinds of changes that occurred with respect to religion. Religion now has access to the media; there is some recognition of the major religious holidays; some confiscated property has been returned; religious education (maybe inside state schools, but more likely outside of them) is permitted; previously banned churches, like the Uniates, are recognized. Furthermore, state supervision of religion through special departments is discontinued, and so presumably is penetration of the hierarchy by the secret police. Charitable and welfare work is positively encouraged. Above all, there is anxiety about the empty spaces of meaning and purpose, and some hope that faith will hold back the spread of superstition and nihilism.

In the early stages of partial democratization, religion acquired some influence in the new leaderships and new Parliaments. Boris Yeltsin carefully attends the Easter celebration of the Orthodox Church as some acknowledgement of the voting power of the faithful. For that matter, Orthodox worship returned to the Kremlin itself. Christian Democratic Parties and Social Unions made their appearance in Eastern Europe, including Russia itself. The Christian Democrats were successful in East Germany, though that is a special case. They had some success in Slovenia and Slovakia, and a Christian

Democratic coalition was initially successful in Hungary. In the Czech Republic, however, they failed. These were not church parties as such, but rather pressure groups that included in their briefs a sympathetic interest in religion.

Most striking was the emergence of leaders who had explicit religious commitments and were virtually non-political. Professor Tadeusz Mazowiecki was, as it turned out, too non-political and modest to survive for long. President Landsbergis was an example of the kind of man briefly emerging at the point of transition. He was an academic, learned in musicology and concerned with the Lithuanian musical tradition. Landsbergis was a Christian, who before one of his historic visits to Moscow, went openly to pray in Vilnius cathedral. Lothar de Maizière, first Prime Minister of East Germany in the first free elections, was a devout Lutheran and his minister of defence was a 'dissident' Lutheran pastor. The first Prime Ministers of Slovenia and Hungary were both devout Catholics; and the Prime Minister of Bosnia (whatever that entity eventually becomes) is a committed Muslim. Even the antagonists in the civil strife in Georgia were of some religious interest. Ghamsakurdia was the type of intellectual who nourished a passionate commitment to national literary renaissance, alongside membership of a religious order. For his part, Shevardnadze recognized the place of religion in Georgia by having himself baptized as 'George'.

Vaclav Havel is of special interest since he is neither Protestant nor Catholic, but was influenced by a Catholic priest while the two of them were in prison. He symbolizes an alliance of some liberals and Catholics through Charter 77 and went after his inauguration to St Vitus

Cathedral in Prague to receive a blessing. At Christmas 1989, he called, in his own words, for a return to 'traditional Christian virtues' as a supportive base for a genuinely civil and honest society. He has even made honesty part of his political programme. It is as if the establishment of a hyper-Machiavellian 'lie' elicits a public demand for truthfulness or at least for a historical court of appeal where truth, not power, is the arbiter. (I personally remember in Romania being asked if I 'still believed in the myth of objectivity' and replying that it was my – and his – last line of defence.)

Since 1989–90 there has been substantial disillusionment and the skilled operators of the old system have made a partial come-back in national guise, especially in Romania, Serbia and Croatia. In the sometime GDR in particular, they have successfully exploited grievances. Many religious leaders in the GDR, Poland and Romania have always been less than eager to sample the fruits of the West which they regard as decadent or materialistic. One priest enquired of me whether the West had any 'goods' to export apart from condoms and pornography. Prophets like Solzhenitsyn are now pushed to declare concrete policies rather than to be luminous beacons of dissent. The religious 'sign' warns and celebrates, but cannot deliver five-year plans.

What of the events of 1989, which even now must astonish us, armed though we should be with realism, caution and some proper fear for the future? This account focuses on key elements in selected countries – East Germany, Hungary, Czechoslovakia, Romania and Yugoslavia – yet giving a little more space to East Germany, because it illustrates the remarkable role played in a secular society by a Church representing no more than one person in five, perhaps much less. In East Germany the Lutheran Church was the single most important conduit of change, alongside the theatre and music. That in itself is indicative: the covert sign languages of music, theatre and faith carry the underground messages until they can surface. (When I carried out research in Bulgaria in 1967 I was told that religion in Sofia University was confined largely to those practising the two languages, music and physics, at a maximum distance from political control and ideological manipulation.)

In East Germany after the late 1940s, to be a believer was very costly. Christians had few job prospects and restricted access to higher education. They were defined as prisoners of a bourgeois ideology (just as the violin was defined as a bourgeois instrument when compared with the accordion). However, in the 1970s there were some relaxations. The government became more responsive to international opinion, and also decided it would be internationally politic to rehabilitate Luther to some degree. The Church was allowed to run discussion groups, though with a very restricted agenda. Christians looked for a focus of religious identity that did not give rise to confrontation, and they found it in the contrast between love and reconciliation and government propaganda in favour of violence and class warfare. Christians also participated in the 'green' movement. They embraced environmental concerns, and found themselves in some danger as a result, since by definition pollution was officially confined to capitalist countries.

By the late 1980s the agenda of these groups had widened. Anyone could join, whether a committed Christian or otherwise. Inevitably there was increased surveillance by the STASI, which could hardly have been difficult in a society where one person in three had some contact with the STASI – including many members and officials of the Church. Church leaders even began to fear massive repression in response to the increasing boldness of the 'Christian' groups. But, in any case, by 1989 the whole nation was in crisis and the Church found itself entering into confidential talks with the government as virtually the only autonomous institution with a representative role, apart from Kurt Masur and the Berlin Philharmonic. Church leaders were used to convey warnings of massive violence and a potential Tiannamen Square if demonstrations did not stop. However, the refusal of Gorbachev to allow the intervention of Red Army tanks probably stayed the hand of the party leadership.

At this point, the Church decided to go openly to the people, preaching the need for non-violent changes and genuine dialogue. The Nikolaikirche in Leipzig became a lantern for several peaceful candlelit processions. These began in prayer, meditation and the music of Bach, and spilled over into vast demonstrations of 100,000 or more. The crowds were monitored by lay people to help ensure their peaceability and to avoid giving any provocation whatever to the tanks that were actually assembled ready in the side streets. At this point, many of the church leaders tried to persuade people to stay in the country and help create a new order, specifically in East Germany. But the dominant mood was to migrate or unite with the Bundesrepublik. At that point, the Wall came down and Rostropovich flew to play Bach's unaccompanied cello suites on the remaining ramparts. In this way, the music of a composer from Thuringia provided as powerful a sign of a universal civilization as Havel's entry into the Gothic shrine of St Vitus on Castle Hill in Prague. However, the channel of the Church through which the tide had pushed was now partly redundant. East Germany, after the Nazi and communist years, was a society that hardly knew what Christianity was. Most people barely recognized the 'sign'. The liveliest religious sector was the Roman Catholic Church, which had cultivated its own plot and pursued strategies of survival as a minority of less than one in ten.

Curiously enough, the minority Protestant tradition in Hungary was also quiescent in the communist period. Indeed, at an early stage it even provided a senior member of the government. Perhaps the Catholic Church had historically been too dominant for Protestants to join with it in opposition. Perhaps the Protestant Church even saw itself in the role of carrier of Hungarian nationalism over against an overarching Austro-Hungarian Catholicism. Kossuth, the hero of 1848, was of Protestant stock. Yet whatever the explanation for this quiescence, the Catholic Church probably mishandled its militant opposition. It had a vast stake in the country, particularly in education, and in the course of a head-on collision it was virtually reduced to a private association and its leadership decapitated. Catholicism was identified as a bourgeois front in league with the USA. In the later years of communism, a traumatized Church veered in the direction of too much compromise, a fact that cost it some prestige in the movement for democracy and hence in post-communist Hungary. State control and infiltration of the Church meant that spiritual impulses took a dissident route. Young people met in small cells and evolved a democratic version of Christianity with a strong interest in peace that ran counter to the hierarchy as well as the government. At the same time, there was a more extensive return to religion dating from the mid-1970s, the meaning of which is disputed. Certainly figures of belief and practice started to rise until at the end of the period a religious minority had become a majority. Whether this is (or was) a revival *de novo* or a return of the repressed seems difficult to say.

A key area in Hungary was education. Church schools had been mostly confiscated and the children of known believers were not allowed to become teachers. The intellectual elites of education and communication provided a site where rival groups battled for control. First the Marxists, humanists and technocrats acquired unstable dominance, at the expense of the old elites, and then there emerged a powerful sector of technologically minded modernizers. With the collapse of communism, some of the modernizers, plus some Marxists, came together to prevent a reassertion of religion. For them it represented the archaic past inimical to progress. The situation was confused because a Christian Democratic coalition emerged victorious in the first free elections. The government offered subsidies to the Church, and pursued a 'Christian national' policy, but attempts at a full-scale restoration encountered strong opposition. The emotions of the previous decades – that is, from the inter-war period and following the holocaust and the time of communist domination – were very strong, both for and against.

The present religious situation in Hungary since the arrival of the centre-left coalition government of 1994 is not strictly of concern here, but it does illustrate the kind of confusion that has followed the communist period, both ecclesiastically and politically. The Churches are moral pressure groups and sources of social critique and social assistance, but there are major issues awaiting resolution, especially the degree of freedom from central state control in education, but also the return of former church property and church financing. The attitude of the Hungarian government at the moment has been described as one of 'positive separation', which means some mutual recognition and some partnership within a framework of ideological neutrality.

In Czechoslovakia (now the Czech Republic and Slovakia) there were two traditions: the liberal secularist one in Czech Lands that had some genealogical root in Reformation Protestantism, and the Catholic one in Slovakia. In Czech Lands the Catholic Church was reimposed in the seventeenth century, and was often viewed as foreign and opposed to national aspirations. In Slovakia, however, the Catholic Church was aligned with nationalist feeling. It is the existence of such different traditions that, among other things, brought about the separation of the two countries following 1989.

At any rate, in Czech Lands the Catholic Church was not initially well placed to resist communism, which had in any case genuine democratic support among the people. However, as the regime revealed its true nature and the democratic movement of 1968 was crushed, an underground emerged that combined secular and religious resistance. Eventually some of the massive losses initially sustained by the Church were reversed. In particular, large crowds gathered for pilgrimages and celebrations of saints prominent in the establishment of Christianity, and the Catholic Church slowly regained autonomy and could replenish its leadership. However, the movement for change in Prague was only in a minor way religiously motivated. At one point the crowds were asked to say the Lord's Prayer, but there were many who no longer knew it. Yet the public celebration in St Vitus did bring together traditions that had historically been deeply antagonistic; and in a way, it was a major achievement of communism to rehabilitate the Roman Catholic Church. A major figure in the rehabilitation was Cardinal Tomasek who, in spite of initial criticism of the Charter 77 group, emerged in the 1980s as a proponent of democratic change.

Whereas in Czechoslovakia it was the Catholic segment of the country that felt itself behind, in (the former) Yugoslavia it was the Catholic segment that felt itself ahead. The Serbs might be the largest group and have a grip on power and on the army, but the Croats and Slovenes lay in the cultural sphere of Central Europe. Yugoslavia was the country through which ran the major divides of East and West, Byzantium and Rome, Austro-Hungary and the Ottomans, and – in some areas – Christian and Muslim. And all the divides had some sort of territorial and ethnic base, though these were intermingled above all in Bosnia, and parts of Croatia, but also in Kosovo and what is now Macedonia. Kosovo is a Londonderry: symbolically and religiously precious to the Serbs, but beleaguered by the local demographic majority of Muslim Albanians.

This area offers the clearest examples of the darker possibilities of ethno-religious strife between mixed populations across ill-defined frontiers. The ex-communists of Serbia have wrapped themselves in ethnic nationalism. They define themselves as the core of sometime Yugoslavia, seek a maximalist version of Greater Serbia, and do so in partial alliance with the Serbian Orthodox Church. The religious elements that accompanied the emergence of Croatia and Serbia from the break-up of Yugoslavia were essentially in alliance with ethnicity, or with imputed ethnicity. The situation is, therefore, very different from that existing in East Germany.

Albania abuts former Yugoslavia, and is itself a religiously divided country, with Catholics in the north, Orthodox in the south, and a Muslim majority (mainly converted by the eighteenth century) in the middle. On All Souls Day 1990, a Catholic priest conducted a baptism, which had up till then been an illegal act. He found that a crowd of 4,000 had gathered, including Muslims apparently, and he was asked to celebrate the Eucharist. At about the same time, the local population dug up bells that had been buried since the prohibition of all religious acts, and hung them on trees to ring in the wind. A premonition of future problems between the Muslim majority and Christian minorities is to be found in the building of new mosques in the semi-Catholic north using Middle Eastern money.

The role of religion was clearly evident over the whole of Eastern Europe from Romania to the Caucasus. Romania provided one of the most interesting cases because it was administered by the peculiar tyranny of the Ceausescu family. The rule of Ceausescu was the nearest approximation in modern times to the achievements of Vlad the Impaler, more widely known as Dracula. Ceausescu did, as a matter of fact, admire and emulate the style of Vlad, and that fact is some indication of his admixture of Marxism, nationalism and megalomanic sadism.

The Romanian Church had negotiated some kind of

modus vivendi with the government from the beginning of communist rule in the late 1940s, and though the Communist Party oppressed the Church, infiltrated and indoctrinated it, there was nevertheless a working alliance cemented by a common Romanian nationalism. This worked to the detriment of the minority groups, which included the Hungarians (mainly Reformed and Catholic) and the voluntary denominations, mainly Baptist and Pentecostal, which had begun to expand rapidly in the 1970s. All the minorities, ethnic and religious and ethno-religious, were concentrated in the north-west, in Transylvania and the Banat.

Ceausescu, in company with his wife Elena, planned to uproot Romanian culture by tearing up Bucharest and by replacing village life with concrete agro-towns. This objective, said to involve the destruction of 14,000 villages, offered the additional pay-off of eliminating the culture of the 2 million Hungarians. However, opposition to Ceausescu on grounds of human rights and minority rights was voiced by Lazlo Tokes, an Hungarian Reformed pastor in Timisoara. An attempt to arrest Tokes failed through the intervention of his congregation and a dissident crowd built up that eventually made for the Opera Square facing the cathedral. In the confrontations that followed, a crowd of perhaps a quarter of a million faced the military and were fired at with the loss of many hundreds of lives. Today the places where they died are marked by crosses in front of the opera house and the cathedral. A second and equally large crowd built up a day or two later and this time faced tanks massed on either side of the cathedral. Many in the crowd knelt and said the Lord's Prayer. Suddenly the tanks turned and trundled away leaving the townspeople in charge of the city. The mayor declared Timisoara a free city from the balcony of the opera house, and was followed there by Pentecostal and Baptist ministers. They cried 'God exists' to responsive cries from the crowd of 'God exists'.

The seismic tremors spread from Timisoara to Sibiu and to Bucharest, where the same pattern of confrontation was reported: shootings, the impromptu erection of crosses, the symbolism of flowers and candles, confusion and the eventual switch of the Army from support for the regime to opposition. Ceausescu and his wife were eventually caught, tried on the spot, and shot on Christmas Day. The balcony from which Ceausescu had given so many speeches to orchestrated (and recorded) cheers was decorated with Christmas trees, bells were rung in every church, carols were sung on television for the first time in decades, and Romanian news announced 'The tyrant has died on Christmas Day'.

What is particularly important about these astonishing events is that the 'signs' of Christianity could be used as part of a mass protest even though institutional Christianity in the form of the majority Church had been largely expropriated. Moreover, there is an interesting contrast with earlier movements of romantic nationalist enthusiasm. For those earlier movements, the Church was simply an element in the national culture, whereas for those who took part in the events of December 1989 it provided the heart of the symbolic repertoire. Today the visitor to the main square in Sibiu sees a monument to the nationalism of the nineteenth century newly surmounted by a cross and candles burning in front of the names of the dead. Naturally the repertoire of protest was not entirely Christian. People sang the old national song and waved the Romanian flag with the communist escutcheon torn out of the middle. But as moral revulsion sought a form, it found the sign language of Christianity to hand.

The story of Poland is too well known for retelling here, and extends over a long period from the killings in Gdansk and the erection of memorial crosses there to the events of the late 1980s. However, two less well-known stories are worth recounting of the events in Lithuania and Georgia.

In April 1989 a vast crowd gathered in the main square of Tiblisi, Georgia, anticipating the dawn of independence with prayers and dancing into the early hours of the morning. Eventually, at about 4 a.m., the Patriarch appeared and was greeted with cries of 'For God, for independence and for Georgia'. Meanwhile the Russian army had assembled only a short distance away and a message was conveyed to the Patriarch to ask the crowds to disperse. He did, but nobody moved. The army advanced into the square and a girl dressed in white and armed with flowers walked towards them saying, 'What are you doing?' The foremost soldier clubbed her to death and, in the mayhem that followed, 19 people died. In the days following, the square filled with flowers, crosses and candles. The suspicion grew that the soldiers had been drugged and had used gas. Eventually a Requiem Mass was held in the patriarchal church attended by thousands, but many left the building choking because the assembled bodies in a confined space gave off noxious fumes.

In the late 1980s a large crowd gathered outside the cathedral of Vilnius, Lithuania, which had previously been turned into a museum. The archbishop entered the church for the first time in many years and lay prostrate before the altar. In the same cathedral in April 1988, a man lay in a cruciform position for 32 days to obtain the release of state prisoners. On All Souls Day of the same year, Mass was broadcast from the cathedral for the first time, and 20,000 people walked to the grave of Jonas Basanavicius, who drafted the Lithuanian Declaration of Independence in 1918. Above Vilnius, there once stood three crosses, central to Lithuanian identity, which were removed at the beginning of the Russian occupation. One of the first acts of independence was to re-erect the crosses.

Everywhere the revolution was forwarded through the making of signs and the retrieval of signs. In Russia itself, Leningrad became St Petersburg again, and the Eucharist returned to the Kremlin. The Kazan cathedral and the cathedral of Christ the Saviour, symbolically demolished by Stalin at the centre of Moscow, were symbolically rebuilt. All over Europe the signs changed, the massive sculptures of the Marxist era were removed, the dead at the hands of the state memorialized, and the city names and street names altered. The main street behind the town square in Sibiu, Romania, is now Metropolitan Street.

The marginal took centre stage and reoccupied sacred space for the liminal period that inaugurated change. It was also proleptic in that religious signs gave advance notice of what was going to happen. A movement for an autocephalous Macedonian Church speaks volumes about the future arrival of independence in general. As change is consummated, the religious signs retire again to their allotted place.

The revolutions of 1989–90, partial as they were bound to be, were more peaceable than any before in history, except maybe the Glorious Revolution of 1688–9, which was in any case more like a coup d'état. Indeed, on 16 February 1989 Cardinal Sladkevicius invoked Gandhi in an example Lithuanians should follow. The chain of 2 million people that formed a human chain from Tallinn to Vilnius, summoned by church bells, was intended as a form of moral force. Except in Poland, the movement hardly seemed even to have leaders. Certain people emerged who stood up for what people wanted. It was not even a question of representing *the* people, denominated by the dangerous definite article, but of an aggregate of persons. These persons were armed solely with signs, and sought to retrieve sacred space at the heart of their common existence. They peaceably invested and reoccupied the public square. Among all the retrievals sought, religion was of paramount importance because it alone, however much suppressed and infiltrated, was by nature an autonomous area, governed by other criteria than force, and speaking an intimate and familial language, not a language of process. A cartoon published at the time showed a hammer smashing itself on an Easter egg.

In a period of European history when one dogma is unlikely to occupy the central square for long, unchallenged Marxism was installed as public truth. As such, it rejected the conversation essential to civil society and pushed religion to the margin and the private sphere. I saw much evidence of that when in 1967 I visited Bulgaria, one of the most secular societies of Europe. I saw the hen coops in which Catholic priests eked out their existence and I ascended stairs through excrement to talk to the wives of pastors gaoled for the previous 20 years. I also visited the empty shell of the

Sephardic synagogue, a relic of another expulsion to a distant margin. During this time I asked my Marxist guide if any dialogue ever occurred between Marxists and believers, and he replied that truth cannot converse with superstition. It is such an approach that has ensured that St Nedeljas church once again stands in St Nedeljas Square, and not in Lenin's.

What happened in Eastern (and Central) Europe has to do with a desire to recover and retain spaces not expropriated by the central powers of the state. There was a time when sacred spaces were themselves locked into the embrace of these powers, and their autonomy compromised, though one could always appeal to the deeper meanings they represented. That meant that a different rhetoric had to carry the burden of autonomy. But once sacred spaces were made marginal by edict of secular dogma, their meaning once more opened up for general use, and they became bases for symbolic challenges to the 'powers of this world'.

Sometimes a mere architectural presence was symbol enough, which is why Stalin systematically demolished so many cathedrals and why Ceausescu tore the heart out of Bucharest and proposed blocking the view of Timisoara Orthodox Cathedral. The point is that, at the very minimum, such buildings have an inalienable transcendental reference which is their sole raison d'être. If that transcendental reference could be compromised, nobody could take their stand on such a ground, literally or intellectually. As the tanks turned away in Timisoara, the Protestant pastor shouted 'God exists' – not because he had witnessed a miracle, but because in the face of triumphant evil one retains a faith that it does not have the last word.

The walk-outs and walk-ins were peaceful so far as was possible. In Lithuania, one of the first signs of a walk-out appeared at a scholarly conference on church music. The people who 'stood out' on such peaceful walks, in Bucharest, or Vilnius or Sofia, were not for the most part political organizers or any kind of political animal. They were playwrights, conductors, musicologists, teachers, pastors and priests, and many of their rallying points were places like churches remote from the eventful world of efficient causes. Somehow the so-called superstructure has a reserve power to affect the sub-structure, and in doing so converted a world where 'the beginning of criticism is the criticism of religion' to one where the beginning of criticism – though not its end – was undertaken by religion.[1]

Note

1. In the above chapter I have not provided annotation, but I wish to acknowledge the usefulness of material by Christel Lane, Timothy Garton Ash, Petra Ramet, Trevor Beeson, Mark Almond, Patrick Michel, Daniel Antal, Petya Nitzova, George Weigel, Michael Bourdeaux, Irene Laumenskaite, Miklos Tomka, Krzysztof Kosela, Attila Molnar, Peter Hebblethwaite, Barbara Strassberg, Janice Brown, Bohdan Bociurkiw, José Casanova and Ivan Varga. Since the chapter makes no attempt to provide a comprehensive frame covering the issues of modernization and post-modernity, I would refer those interested in particular to Patrick Michel (1991) *Politics and Religion in Eastern Europe* (Oxford, Polity Press).

FURTHER READING

Latin America

Adriance, Madeleine (1995) *Promised Land. Base Communities and the struggle for the Amazon* (Albany, New York, State University of New York Press).

Appleby, Scott and Martin Marty (eds) (1991) *Fundamentalisms Observed* (Chicago, Chicago University Press).

Bastian, Jean-Pierre (1994) *Le Protestantisme en Amérique Latine* (Geneva, Labor et Fides).

Blumhofer, Edith (1993) *Restoring the Faith* (Urbana, University of Illinois Press).

Burdick, John (1994) *Looking for God in Brazil:The Progressive Church in Urban Brazil* (Berkeley, University of California Press).

Burnett, Virginia Garrard and David Stoll (eds) (1993) *Rethinking Protestantism in Latin America* (Philadelphia, Temple University Press).

Cleary, Edward and Hannah Stewart-Gambino (1994) *Conflict and Competition* (London and Boulder, Lynne Rienner).

Cook, Guillermo (1985) *The Expectation of the Poor: Latin American Basic Ecclesial Communities in Protestant Perspective* (Maryknoll, Orbis Books).

Cotton, Ian (1995) *The Hallelujah Revolution. The Rise of the New Christians* (London, Little, Brown).

Cox, Harvey (1994) *Fire from Heaven: Pentecostalism, Spirituality, and the Rethinking of Religion in the Twenty-First Century* (New York, Addison-Wesley).

D'Epinay, Christian Lalive (1969) *Haven to the Masses* (London, Lutterworth Press).

Droogers, Andre and Susanna Rostas (eds) (1993) *The Popular Use of Popular Religion in Latin America* (Amsterdam, CEDLA and Free University).

Freston, Paul (1994) 'Popular Protestants in Brazilian Politics', in *Religion and Politics in Brazil, Social Compass*, 41:4.

Harrison, Larry (1992) *Who Prospers? How Cultural Values Shape Economic and Political Success* (New York, Basic Books).

Haynes, Jeff (1993) *Religion in Third World Politics* (Buckingham and Philadelphia, Open University Press).

Hewitt, William (1991) *Base Christian Communities and Social Change in Brazil* (Lincoln, University of Nebraska Press).

Hollenweger, Walter (1972) *The Pentecostals: The Charismatic Movement in the Churches* (Minneapolis, Augsburg Publishing).

Ireland, Rowan (1992) *Kingdoms Come: Religion and Politics in Brazil* (Pittsburgh, Pittsburgh University Press).

Martin, David (1990) *Tongues of Fire. The Explosion of Protestantism in Latin America* (Oxford, Basil Blackwell).

Poewe, Karla (1994) *Charismatic Christianity as a Global Culture* (Columbia, SC, University of South Carolina Press).

Poloma, Margaret (1989) *The Assemblies of God at the Crossroads* (Knoxville, University of Tennessee Press).

Stoll, David (1990) *Is Latin America Turning Protestant? The Politics of Evangelical Growth* (Berkeley, University of California Press).

Veliz, Claudio (1994) *The New World of the Gothic Fox* (Berkeley, University of California Press).

Willems, Emilio (1967) *Followers of the New Faith* (Nashville, Vanderbilt University Press).

Wilson, Bryan (1973) *Magic and the Millennium* (London, Heinemann).

Eastern Europe

Anderson, John (1994) *Religion, State and Politics in the Soviet Union and the Successor States* (Cambridge, Cambridge University Press).

Antal, Daniel (1994) *Out of Romania* (London, Faber).

Ash, Timothy Garton (1985) *The Polish Revolution: Solidarity* (Sevenoaks, Hodder).

Ash, Timothy Garton (1990) *The Uses of Adversity: Essays on the Fate of Central Europe* (New York, Vintage Books).

Beeson, Trevor (1974) *Discretion and Valour* (London, Fontana).

Bociurkiw, Bohdan and John Strong (1975) *Religion and Atheism in the USSR and Eastern Europe* (London, Macmillan).

Bourdeaux, Michael (1970) *Patriarchs and Prophets* (New York, SCM Press).

Gannon, Thomas (1988) *Catholicism in Transition* (contains introductory essay by David Martin and useful essays on Hungary and Poland) (London, Macmillan).

Havel, Vaclav *et al.* (1990) *The Power of the Powerless: Citizens against the State in Central-Eastern Europe* (Armonk, M. E. Sharpe).

Johnston, H. (1993) 'Religio-Nationalist Sub-Cultures under the Communists', *Sociology of Religion*, 54(3), pp. 237–55.

Kubiak, Jerome (1970) *Religiosity and Social Milieu* (Warsaw, Polish Academy).

Lane, Christel (1978) *Christian Religion in the Soviet Union* (London, Allen & Unwin).

Lane, Christel (1981) *The Rites of Rulers – Ritual in Industrial Society* (Oxford, Oxford University Press).

Marshall, Ruth H. (ed.) (1971) *Aspects of Religion in the Soviet Union 1917–1967* (Chicago, Chicago University Press).

Martin, David (1969) 'The Bulgarian Ideology', in *The Religious and the Secular* (London, Routledge).

Michel, Patrick (1992) *Les Religions à L'Est* (Paris, Cerf).

Michel, Patrick (1994) *Politique et Religion: La Grande Mutation* (Paris, Alban Michel).

Ramet, Petra (ed.) (1989) *Religion and Nationalism in Soviet and East European Politics* (Durham, NC, Duke University Press).

Ramet, Petra (ed.) (1993) *Religious Policy in the Soviet Union* (Cambridge, Cambridge University Press).

Runciman, Steven (1971) *The Orthodox Churches and the Secular State* (Auckland, Auckland University Press).

Szajkowski, Bogdan (1983) *Next to God – Poland: Politics and Religion in Contemporary Poland* (New York, St Martin's Press).

Tomka, Miklos (1994) 'The Sociology of Religion in Eastern and Central Europe', *Social Compass*, 41:3, pp. 379–92.

Varga, Ivan, Srdjan Urcan and others on Orthodoxy and Modernity in Roberto Cipriani (ed.) (1993) *Religions sans Frontières* (Rome, Department of Information).

Weigel, George (1992) *The Final Revolution* (Oxford, Oxford University Press).